AMERICAN MARTYR,

The Jon Daniels Story

Commemorative Edition

William J. Schneider

MOREHOUSE PUBLISHING
Harrisburg, PA

All royalties from this book will be applied to the Jonathan Myrick Daniels Fellowship Fund, *established by the Trustees of the Episcopal Divinity School to provide financial assistance to seminarians undertaking to strengthen their theological education through participation in social movements concerned with important human needs. The residents of Keene, New Hampshire, made the initial contributions to this Fund, for which the Trustees continue to accept donations.*

Copyright © 1992 by the Episcopal Divinity School

Morehouse Publishing

Editorial Office:
871 Ethan Allen Highway
Ridgefield, CT 06877

Corporate Office:
P.O. Box 1321
Harrisburg, PA 17105

Library of Congress Cataloging-in-Publication Data
Daniels, Jonathan Myrick, 1939-1965.
    American martyr : the Jon Daniels story / [edited by] William J. Schneider.
       p. cm.
    Originally published: The Jon Daniels story. New York : Seabury Press, 1967.
    ISBN 0-8192-1586-4 (pbk.)
    1. Daniels, Jonathan Myrick, 1939-1965. 2. Civil rights workers—United States—Biography. 3. Afro-Americans—Civil rights. 4. Murder—Alabama—Selma Region—History—20th century. I. Schneider, William J. II. Daniels, Jonathan Myrick, 1939-1965. Jon Daniels story. III. Title.
E185.98.D3A3   1993
973.92'092—dc20   92-14126
[b]   CIP

Printed in the United States of America
by
BSC LITHO
Harrisburg, PA 17105

O God of justice and compassion, you put down the proud and mighty from their place, and lift up the poor and the afflicted: We give you thanks for your faithful witness Jonathan Myrick Daniels, who, in the midst of injustice and violence, risked and gave his life for another; and we pray that we, following his example, may make no peace with oppression; through Jesus Christ the just one: who lives and reigns with you and the Holy Spirit, one God, for ever and ever. *Amen.*

The collect for August 14, commemorating Jonathan Myrick Daniels, from *The Lesser Feasts and Fasts 1991,* © The Church Pension Fund, used by permission.

Foreword

The first edition of *The Jon Daniels Story* was in April, 1967. Now toward the close of 1992 comes a second printing—twenty-seven years after Jonathan's death.

The content of this printing is the same as the first edition which had been prepared by Jon's friend, William J. Schneider, then Episcopal chaplain at Harvard and Radcliffe. Nothing has been changed in the book. The changes have come in the readers; the readers' perception of Jon and their deeper understanding of his life and death.

What are some of those changes? One, surely, is that Jon is now recognized as a martyr. The General Convention of the Episcopal Church has voted in the summer of 1991 to include Jonathan in the Church Calendar and given appropriate Propers. He now has his own liturgical day.

This ecclesiastical recognition undoubtedly has helped many who knew Jon (or knew of him) to understand what a martyr is: One who is doing whatever he or she is doing—sometimes very ordinary things—because of the conviction that this is the only way one can respond to God. God is the one who initiates or calls the martyr to action. *What* the action is is not as important as *why* the action. The answer is God.

It is clear that Jonathan made his decision to go to Selma and thus to his death because of his conviction that that was what God wanted him to do. He went to Selma simply because he "had to go." To say—as many have said—that Jon was killed because he was a civil rights worker is, on one hand, true; on the other it is false, or more accurately, inadequate.

The unmistakable conclusion one comes to on re-reading *The Story* after twenty-seven years is that Jon's main concern was not civil rights. It was obedience to Christ and that obedience led to his witness in the area of civil rights and so to his death. In another day and in a different place such obedience might have led to a different vocation: a teacher, a doctor—whatever. He came to be a genuinely authentic Christian person and that was his heart's desire: called to be a saint.

What is clear now in the re-reading of *The Story*—and perhaps the most significant thing about it—is that lives have been changed by Jon's martyrdom. Testimonials to that effect in great numbers—from people who had known Jon, worked with him, played with him, grown up with him, been to school with him or people who had simply read about him—influenced the General Convention to vote *unanimously* for his recognition within the liturgical structure of the church. And countless others—some known, many unknown—have been helped by Jon in his life and death to lead their own lives with some additional grace and courage, with a deepened, more joyful faith in their own pilgrimage.

For all of that hidden strength that has come to us from Jon, our friend and martyr, we thank him, and we thank God.

JOHN B. COBURN

Brewster, Massachusetts
All Saints' Day 1991

Preface

Shortly after Jon Daniels' death in August of 1965, it was suggested that his letters and papers be collected and made available to the reading public. This is not surprising since a number of his friends and colleagues were already familiar with the quality and depth of some of his writings. "A Burning Bush" had been published in the *Episcopal Theological School Journal;* a paper prepared for a theology course was read at his funeral. Both of these moving and perceptive documents have since been reprinted in a number of newspapers and periodicals. Both appear in this present volume.

The search for Jon's letters and other papers was begun in October, 1965, and most of what was forthcoming was in hand by December of that year. Once these materials were assembled, it became clear that some biographical information would be necessary in order to provide a context for Jon's words. The biographical introduction is not intended to supply a complete account of Jon's twenty-six years. It is rather a sketch designed to present the reader with enough background and insight into Daniels' character to make his letters and papers more readily understood and appreciated.

I knew Jon only during the last two years of his life. I was largely dependent upon other people for detailed knowledge of his earlier years. Hours were spent in taped interviews with dozens of persons, only a few of whom can be mentioned by name here. Theresa Roberts, Carlton T. Russell, Richard Snowman, Gray Thoron, Ruth Raymond, Elizabeth Tracy, Harold Drew, Fred Fox, J. Eugene Felch, Frank Foley, William Hazelett, Caroline Howard, and Chandler McCarty acquainted me with Jon's years in Keene, New Hampshire. I am deeply grateful to each of them for their willingness to talk with me about Jon at a time when they were still in shock over his death.

William Braithwaite, Joseph Pearce, George Roth, Herbert Dillard, William Kelly, Josiah Bunting, and James Wilson were largely responsible for helping me to understand Jon's four years at the Virginia Military Institute. I am indebted to Julia Smith Martin of the Public Relations Office there for the research which she did on my behalf and for her prompt replies to my numerous letters and questions. I am grateful to General George Shell for making available to me information necessary to develop an accurate picture of Jon while he was a student at the Institute.

Philip Holliday, Blaney Colmore, and Robert Oakes assisted me in my understanding of the ETS years. Their cooperation was invaluable.

There are several persons without whom this volume would never have appeared, and I wish therefore to single them out for very special thanks:

Judith Upham, for the *many* hours she spent verbally retracing the footsteps that Jon and she walked in Selma

The Rev. Richard Morrisroe, for his willingness to be interviewed for this book from his hospital bed in Chicago, and for his friendship

The Rev. John B. Morris, Executive Secretary of the Episcopal Society for Cultural and Racial Unity, for his constant assistance in collecting letters and taping interviews as well as for his persistent encouragement

The Rev. Maurice Ouellet, the Rev. William J. Wolf, and David Gordon for their guidance, for reading the manuscript, and for making important and helpful comments which improved the text

Deborah Lovejoy, my secretary, for typing and retyping the manuscript and for all of the other tasks she performed in preparing this manuscript for publication

The Rev. John B. Coburn, for writing the Foreword and for making available all of the material and resources of the Episcopal Theological School in order that this book might be written.

W.J.S.

Contents

AMERICAN MARTYR
The Jon Daniels Story

On August 20, 1965, Jon Daniels, a seminary student and volunteer civil rights worker, was shot to death by Tom Coleman, a white deputy sheriff, in front of a "cash" store in Hayneville, Alabama. The killing took place in broad daylight, and the facts surrounding it were amply recorded, indeed broadcast immediately around the world.

The nation was shocked. It had not yet assimilated the news of the killings, just months prior, of the civil rights workers James Reeb and Viola Gregg Liuzzo. Now to those killings, and to the killings of the Negroes and other whites who worked for civil rights, was added that of the seminarian Jon Daniels. The news was almost incredible—but true.

In Keene, New Hampshire, where Jon grew up, and in Cambridge, Massachusetts, at the Episcopal Theological School, where he was a student, there was not only shock but profound grief that the life of one so promising had been senselessly terminated, that the warm, sympathetic person who was Jon Daniels would no longer greet his neighbors, his classmates, his friends.

Who was this young man? What had been his life before it was so abruptly and notoriously snuffed out? Why had he felt compelled to go to Selma, and why, having gone there, did he feel called to return after the fanfare passed and most other "outsiders" had forever departed?

To answer these questions we have brought together here the Jon Daniels story as we have been able to glean it from the memories of his family, his friends, his teachers, his schoolmates, and his associates, as well as from his letters. The story that emerges of that life and that ministry and that absurd death is told because it happened and is part of the meaning of Christian commitment in the life and conflicts of America today.

The Early Years in Keene

Jonathan Myrick Daniels was born in Keene, New Hampshire, March 20, 1939, the only son of Dr. and Mrs. Philip Brock Daniels. Except for the war years when Dr. Daniels was a medical officer in the United States Army, Jon was raised in Keene, where his mother and his Grandmother Weaver still live.

During Dr. Daniels' military service the family resided in the border states, where Jon got his first glimpse of southern life. While in high school, Jon stated, "Although I was only five at the time I retain, with distinct clarity, more memories of that period than of any other time or place since. . . . I think of the South as my adopted home and because of this, I cannot help but sympathize with her—in fact I must confess that I have a great affection, I hope not too disloyal to my country and heritage, for the gallant and valorous, but misguided Johnny Rebs." So it was that at five years of age, quite unknown to Jon Daniels or anyone else, the first steps toward Selma twenty-one years later were already being taken.

During his early years in Keene, Jon was an ordinary boy, though his verbal acumen, his gentlemanly qualities, and his genuine and open friendliness toward persons of all ages were uniquely his own and served to distinguish him.

His mother tells a story about an experience in high school that reveals much about his personality. "A friend of Jon's," as Mrs. Daniels tells the story, "had purchased a car, the insurance for which was to go into effect one November midnight. That was the night of the Community Concert, which Jon never missed. The whole family went. We came home, had coffee, and then went to bed. Well, the next morning Dr. Daniels, who had to be up early, became aware of some very odd sounds emanating from the direction of Jon's room. When he went out to investigate, he found Emily, our daughter, quite upset. It seems that Jon had awakened her at 4:30 A.M., informing her that he couldn't stand it any longer and was in awful agony. He told her his whole story but swore her to secrecy. It seems that the night before, after the 'Good nights' had been said, this friend, per agreement, came over and got a ladder out of our garage and put it up to the roof. Jon made it out and down all right, but while climbing up when he got back, he slipped on the roof—or rather off of it—and fell to the ground. Being November, the earth was hard and frozen. Consequently everything on his left side was either sprained, bruised, strained, or pulled. There wasn't any part of him that didn't hurt. And for most of the next month he was in the hospital recovering."

That time in the hospital seems to have been decisive in Jon's life. He had many hours alone to think. From this time on, without losing his sense of humor and his searing wit, Jon showed a new seriousness that was to remain with him the rest of his life.

It was during the same period that Jon first gave serious consideration to the Roman Catholic Church. He had often talked religion and theology with two friends, Carlton Russell and Eugene Felch. Occasionally he attended Sunday worship at the local Catholic church with Gene. He was struck and moved by the liturgy, especially the drama of the Mass. While recuperating he had had long talks with the pastor of Keene's Roman Catholic parish. Although Jon was never to join the Roman Church, he did leave the Congregational Church of his early days and was confirmed in the Episcopal Church. After deliberation, he concluded that the Congregational Church was too free for him and the Roman Church too rigid. Anglicanism provided the *via media*.

That Jon, even as a high school student, was searching for a deeper understanding of Christianity was reflected in the stories that he wrote for the *Enterprise,* a high school literary magazine, as well as in the conversations he was having with friends and in the books he was reading at the time. Frequently Jon, Gene Felch, and Carlton Russell would go to a friend's home in Dublin, New Hampshire. "We would take a stereo set," Gene Felch recalls, "a lot of good records and some steaks, and spend at least the night there if not the weekend. We would talk about philosophy, history, what was going on in the world, and the intellectual and religious problems we were facing." Carlton Russell recalls: "Jon was intense, spontaneously interested in and warm toward others, razor-sharp in conversation, aware of the entire gamut of experience from the obscene to the divine. . . ."

It appears that Jon had also given thought to his academic standing in high school, while he was in the hospital. Until then he was doing little better than average work except in English where he was a "natural." After his accident this changed and when he graduated he held membership in the National Honor Society.

The question of vocation, what he was to do with his life, Jon found to be disturbing and unsettling. For some time he had been considering the ministry, but teaching, medicine, and the law also attracted him at intervals. Mrs. Daniels, a strong yet gentle lady, encouraged Jon to pursue all his interests, criticized his faults, and applauded his successes. She herself was an avid reader and, following her example, Jon became one too. Consequently, his interests were far-reaching: music, drama, literature, the church, politics, and philosophy were all in turn to absorb and excite him.

Jon's primary concern, however, was for people, and it was quite natural that this should be the case. He had been raised in the home of a doctor who, as one of the founders of the Keene Clinic, is to this day remembered for the loyalty, devotion, and love that he bestowed on his patients.

Jon expressed his interest in people in several ways. There was a spontaneous openness, free and uninhibited. A close friend of the family recalls that when he walked down Court Street, Jon would greet with a smile and pleasant word people of all ages and would in turn be hailed by the tooting horns of others as they drove by. A former teacher, Miss Elizabeth Tracy, has this recollection: "My route home and Jon's were more or less parallel. Jon would always join me and take whatever packages I had. If we met some friends of his, he would always stop and introduce them—something most younger people simply would not do."

Jon's friendliness would also reach out, sometimes consciously but often unconsciously, to the person in need. His high school principal remembers him well: "Jon was always a champion of the underdog. If some kid was in trouble, Jon would plead for him. He was also a champion of lost causes. If in school he felt that an injustice had been done somewhere, possibly he thought disciplinary action was unjust or that a teacher was unjust or that certain of the students were unjust to other students, Jon was upset and immediately involved in trying to get the matter straightened out. He had a tremendous liking for people in generic terms —just plain people."

Generally speaking, Jon's classmates respected him and appreciated his friendly openness. There were some, however, for whom his gentlemanly behavior was a source of amusement; others were irritated and not infrequently alienated by his nonconformist positions.

Other aspects of Jon's character were to manifest themselves in the short stories he wrote for his high school magazine the *Enterprise*. In all these stories he was exploring the meaning of life and death. His interest in these themes can to a degree be attributed to the normal experience and searching of adolescence; in part, also, to the fact that as a doctor's son, the issues of life and health, sickness and death, were part of his everyday experience at home. In addition, there was Jon's own deepening awareness that at the heart of his faith is a death on a cross. Death, then, had for Jon an immediacy that was unusual in a person of his age. His story "In Memoriam" (1955) tells—almost prophetically —of a young priest who was shot in the act of helping someone he loved. In "The Stranger" Jon wrestled with the problem of evil in a Joblike narrative about a soldier who returned from war to discover that his home and family had been destroyed by fire. Jon's other stories have similar themes.

Jon's friendliness, his concern for the victim of injustice, his brooding interest in the meaning of life and death as well as his curious attraction to the South—all more or less dissociated during these early years in Keene—were, we know now, to merge later in an extraordinary and public conclusion.

The Years at Virginia Military Institute

After graduation from high school, Jon entered, at Lexington, Virginia, the Virginia Military Institute (VMI), a military liberal-arts college that aims to produce the "citizen-soldier." In the light of Jon's interests in high school, his thoughts about the ministry, and his physical slightness, his choice seemed an unlikely one.

It puzzled also his classmates at VMI. One cadet later explained it this way:

"At seventeen, Jon's ideas about the future were unsettled. The military can have a strange attraction for a young man with imagination, especially if the young man is rather small and skinny, and wants to complement what he takes to be his own intellectual bent with a certain toughness." One member of the VMI faculty tells of a conversation Jon had with his wife in which he told her he wanted to be sure he "had the makings of a man," that he looked to VMI to provide him with physical tolerance.

According to fellow classmates at the Institute, Jon was not particularly happy there, at least at the beginning. He datelined a letter to Gene Felch during his first year "Hell, Thursday, October 10," and wrote, "What with 'bracing' [a rigid and painful position of attention], all the abuse from upperclassmen, and too much studying to be done in too little time—in short, a perpetual rat race—the life of a Rat is somewhat less than ethereal bliss."

Other classmates had similar impressions. "I found Jon to be a man of distinct contrasts through our three years as roommates. Initially I thought that he was definitely at the wrong school, based primarily on his attitude toward the military schedule, his general appearance physically, and his high degree of sensitiveness toward criticism directed at him, a daily occurrence during the two years as underclassman. At first he assumed a distant, if not hostile, attitude toward the southern student—definitely in the majority— and took great pride, bordering on the snobbish, in being a member of the Yankee minority. Yet, as school went on, the greater part of his confidants were Southerners. Jon was a fiercely proud individual, confident of his abilities, aware of his shortcomings, and, although not at first, he was tolerant of the shortcomings of others. Academically Jon's record speaks for itself. . . ."

Another classmate has given us this sketch: "The Virginia Military Institute was not the kind of school where one would expect to find a man like Jon Daniels. He seemed simply out of place there. He spoke softly; he looked, and probably was, frail physically. He was 'intellectual.' In fact, most of us who came to know him, in that bleak fall of 1957, considered him rather effeminate. Appearances deceive, however, and Jon's did. When you spoke with him you forgot his frailness, his seeming effeminacy and weakness. His words were strong; there was nothing frail about his ideas, nor—even more—about his willingness to admit his error if it were shown him in a clear debate. It always seemed that he was able to see human frailty, including his own, with too much clarity for his own good. This may have been his greatest weakness."

Weakness or not, Jon opposed much of the routine among the students, especially the "military" rigors of VMI, and as an upperclassman, he was known as a "Rat Daddy" for his help to first-year students, who are known as "Rats" at the Institute.

At the beginning of sophomore year Jon's faith began to wane, probably because it was, for the first time, seriously challenged. Skepticism, characteristic of college life, forced itself in upon him, and his intentions about a Christian ministry turned toward teaching. His church attendance became sporadic even though Sunday church attendance is required at VMI. During his years in Keene no one had seriously challenged his religious beliefs or his vocation for the ministry. His best friends in Keene, Carlton Russell and Gene Felch, largely concurred in Jon's religious ideas, and clergymen and other adults in the community encouraged him in his interests.

As with any college freshman Jon was confronted at VMI with a diversity of moral standards and spiritual commitments, and like most freshmen he had his period of doubting. As one friend put it: "One would guess that a small New Hampshire town had not confronted him with the diversity of moral standards and spiritual commitments that any college freshman sees among his fellows. It was not that Jon was naïve; it was that he was inexperienced, and these are not the same." This doubt also affected his thinking about the ministry. A former VMI faculty member recalls a meeting with Jon during this time period: "One rainy afternoon in the fall of 1958 Jon dropped by my office, and while we were chatting politely, I asked him about his general aim for the future. He replied, 'The Episcopal ministry.' I then asked him the reason for his decision, not negatively, just out of curiosity. Jon began to state his reasons. First—well, people expected it of him—the folks back home in Keene. Secondly, he was basically afraid. He didn't trust himself in the world, he didn't think like the world, he hardly understood it, and he didn't trust its reaction to him or his to it. There were just lots of games that he didn't care to play, and the ministry looked like a safe and quiet way to read, study, have congenial friends, etc. He didn't want much and the little he wanted it could provide. On this line he rambled for a while. But he got more involved and became more negative. I simply rode along on a tide of words wondering what next. He finally admitted to real qualms about the whole deal. He didn't know why he was thinking of the ministry. He didn't even know that he believed in anything. At any rate, he decided the Episcopal Church game was not for him and left that afternoon quite charged up with some new-found freedom. I had literally done nothing except provide a sounding board—though I was marked thereafter as the Devil's disciple."

As his faith waned, Jon's interest in the existentialists, in the Theater of the Absurd, in literature which explores the meaninglessness of our age grew and with it a curious fascination—almost an obsession—with death. Short stories he wrote during his VMI years reflect the shift in his concern: no *deus ex machina,* no saving Jesus, no purpose or joy in life, but in their place emptiness, meaninglessness, despair, suicide, and death.

During his junior year at VMI, Jon's father died, after a long, painful terminal illness that deepened Jon's doubts about the Christian faith. Questions that were to plague him for several years flooded into his mind: Why should a good man die so early and painful a death? What justice is there in this universe? What does it all mean?

During his junior year, and perhaps as a tribute to his father, Jon began to take science courses with the thought of preparing for a medical career, possibly in psychiatry, although in his senior year he was again devoting his major attention to English literature. Also, as a consequence of his father's death, Jon had to assume new responsibilities toward his family. Within months his sister became seriously ill and her medical costs proved beyond Mrs. Daniels' means. Jon therefore worked the following summer to help cover both personal and family expenses.

Senior year at VMI brought Jon high academic and personal recognition. He was awarded both a Woodrow Wilson and a Danforth Fellowship for graduate study. He commanded the respect of everyone who knew him and was known to be honest, outspoken, talented. As a mark of their recognition his classmates elected him Valedictorian of the First Class, a high honor and an unusual one for an English major.

In his valedictory speech Jon noted the following feelings and reactions to VMI: "We say farewell to a mosaic of sensations and impressions which we cannot forget, . . . the metallic click of polished heels, the bugler's canonical hours. We shall miss the Blue Ridge Mountains and the green of the Valley. We are conscious of a host of things, some good and some bad, which have left their mark on us during the past four years. We have not the perspective in many cases to distinguish the good from the bad, the beneficial from the detrimental. It will take years for us to gain that perspective. But that will be in another country, and, as the saying goes, the wench will be dead. Every man who is graduated today will leave with a sense of regret for *something* at VMI which he has learned to love."

The address concluded: "My colleagues and friends, I wish you the joy of a purposeful life. I wish you new worlds and the vision to see them. I wish you the decency and the nobility of which you are capable. These will come with the maturity which it is now our job to acquire on farflung fields. The only thing we can do at this time . . . is to 'greet the unseen with a cheer.' "

The observations of a former VMI faculty member who counseled Jon in his junior and senior years summarize neatly for us Jon's character at the conclusion of his VMI experience: "My first meeting with Jon Daniels was in the early fall of 1960. . . . He was then, as ever, unassuming, reserved, but intense and responsive in personal relationships. He was very much in the throes of self-discovery, frustrated because he could not then determine whether he wanted to pursue graduate study in English, enter medical school or study for the ministry. Jon had been deeply influenced by others. His professors at VMI, notably people like Col. Herbert Dillard and Col. Carrington Tutwiler, nurtured his talents in English, and he clearly was excited about the possibilities of doing graduate work at Harvard. Yet his social concerns were emerging strongly too, and he felt drawn to the medical profession by the example his father had set. The interest in religion had not clearly defined itself. The *concern* was there all right, more permanently than with most young men. . . . At the same time, Jon was in a period of doubt and skepticism, in no small measure due to his lively philosophical and literary interests. As a man of deep conscience he was troubled because he could not resolve these matters, could not, he felt, even attend church services without feelings of guilt, and because of these doubts I had some difficulty persuading him that he was still quite eligible for a Danforth nomination. Nonetheless, I and others did persuade him. . . ."

Graduate School and Conversion

In the fall of 1961 Jon began graduate study in English literature at Harvard University. During the previous summer he had worked in the Washington office of Senator Norris Cotten of New Hampshire. Life in Washington and the inner workings of government fascinated him. In July he wrote to his mother: "I think it unlikely that I shall ever teach English—or get a doctorate. Law and the associated studies of economics, government and political science (to some extent) seem the best bet." This reaction to his Washington experience was, we might note, quite typical of Jonathan Daniels. Whatever he did, he did intensely and enthusiastically; what he was doing "right now" completely absorbed him and appeared to him to be the center of action.

His year of graduate study at Harvard was a year of anxiety and overwhelming unhappiness, and the inner struggle he was experiencing left him unsettled and exhausted most of the time. His sister's illness also continued to distress him greatly.

Looking back on the period and recalling their correspondence, Jon's friend and former mentor at VMI has stated: "I wrote Jon a harsh letter at the time advising him to hold on and not quit. He would be quitting, I told him, not to go to seminary or anywhere else, but because life was abhorrent to him. He hated Harvard, hated the Latin authors he was having to plow so doggedly through, hated scholarship in general, and hated the world for the grief it seemed to be pouring on his sister and himself. I told him that Nature operated by profusion—that a million efforts, or lives, producing one success was cheap according to nature; that history had no compassion for failure—that only success counted, the rest was simply quietly covered up and forgotten. That the choice was his as to which should happen to him. That he could find, always, an infinite number of reasons for *not* being his true and authentic self, but only *one* reason eternally for *being* his true self. That his decision must be ruthless, based not on 'conditions,'—sisters, mothers, fathers, heredities, or what have you—but on the one illogical and baseless image of his true self which he must be. . . ."

During the year it also became apparent that Jon was having a delayed grief reaction to his father's death. And his mounting misery led him to seek counseling at the Harvard Health Service.

At the same time Jon was occasionally attending services at the Church of the Advent in Boston. Uncertain as to his beliefs, more agnostic than Christian, he was nonetheless drawn to that parish because of his strong response to the music, the drama of the liturgy, and his inherent love for the church and the Eucharist, which, even in his most negative moments, did not desert him. On Easter Sunday, 1962, in the Church of the Advent, Jon had a conversion experience that was to determine the remainder of his life. The details of this conversion experience are not known. Jon would frequently mention it in general terms, but so far as the writer can determine, no one ever heard him describe it in explicit detail. We do know that as a result of his counseling and his discussion of his Harvard experience with others, he concluded that he should not pursue graduate work in English literature. Shortly after his conversion experience he made a firm decision to enter seminary in preparation for the ordained ministry.

The following year, however, was spent at home, working to help with family expenses, continuing his introspective analysis of self, and preparing for admission to the seminary. In the course of the year he held two jobs, one with an electrical concern in Keene, the other as an orderly at Elliott Community Hospital. On the latter he was trained as a surgical technician and had the opportunity of working in surgery directly with doctors. Again, medicine appealed to him as a vocation, but the appeal was not sufficiently strong to alter his decision about the ordained ministry. Some of the conclusions he reached during this year of introspective analysis he ably stated in the "Autobiography" he submitted with his admission application to the Episcopal Theological School, to which he was highly commended by the Bishop of New Hampshire, the Rt. Rev. Charles F. Hall, and by his rector in Keene, the Rev. Chandler H. McCarty.

Seminary Training

The Episcopal Theological School (ETS)[1] in Cambridge, Massachusetts, is a long way from Selma, Alabama. Located on Brattle Street, one of the oldest and most handsomely housed avenues in America, ETS for one hundred years has been committed to the enterprise of educating men for the Christian ministry. Jon Daniels entered ETS in September, 1963, with the expectation of graduating in June, 1966, to undertake a teaching ministry in a college or university. During his first year in seminary he took the usual basic seminary courses. These courses in biblical studies, church history, theology, and Greek he found challenging.

Toward the end of the year, Jonathan wrote to his sister Emily and her husband Vin: "Greek has been going just wretchedly—and it is time to spend a little effort on three other courses. But I am happy, happy, happy—deeply aware of the mercy of God (in whom to summarize a violent year, I am learning to believe

[1]The Episcopal Theological School (ETS) is now the Episcopal Divinity School (EDS) as a result of a 1974 merger with the Philadelphia Divinity School. It is still located in Cambridge.

with the kind of faith that I begin to see Christianity is or ought to be about), humbled by recent experiences which have probed (and begun to redeem?) my defenses and pretenses and wounds, thrilled with life as at last I begin to *see* it. I think I am beginning to discover—through various people, books, gropings towards love in many lives, the Church, the presence of the Risen Lord (not least in the Sacrament), the challenge of pretty exciting Christian thinking and ideas, something 'me-changing' about Christian life and faith. This whole year is the most important of my life to date."

The twelve hours a week Jon spent in the field, under supervision, working in an interracial church program in Providence, Rhode Island, offered him a specific, concrete context within which to test his theological insights and directions. In a Field Work evaluation report he had this comment to make: "Excellent! An introduction to problems of urban society and of the urban church in its ministry. Because of complex relations with various components of the city (slum, underprivileged children, undergraduates, clergy) under naturally evolving conditions of intimacy, the assignment provides a view of the natures of both church and society as they exist concretely. Challenging, tiring, often discouraging with respect to human resources, renewing and crucial to my 'holy' history. It has revised my preconceptions of my own ministry and opened unexpected horizons. . . . The program is invaluable *to me*—experientially, ethically, spiritually. When I came to seminary I planned without qualification to enter the teaching ministry, virtually excluding either the challenge or the value of the parish priesthood and related ministries. Though I cannot make a definitive prophecy at the moment, I am happy (and thankful) to confess that my new horizons are alluring. I believe, specifically, that I could serve my Lord with a glad heart in a slum."

During this first year Jon's progress toward a mature theology was demonstrated in a paper for a New Testament professor, in which he discussed some parables in St. Matthew's Gospel: "The Lord of the Christian's prayers, the Lord of the Church's worship and preaching, is Lord over suffering and the panic of doubt, the Lord of forgiveness and sacrificial love. He is Lord over human bondage to death in all its degrees. . . ." In a subsequent theology examination he developed this thought, describing its implications in terms of human relationships: ". . . as creation is the gracious action of a loving God, man (like everything else) bears in himself the style and character of that God (whom we know in Christ). Man is sinner: yes. But the incredible act of reconciliation, of seeking out the lost sheep at any cost, involved in the Incarnation rather affirms than denies (I believe) the ultimate worth of man to the Father who made him. If that is true, then— to take a long leap—it is imperative that *we* view ourselves (and our neighbors—the Chinese, for example) as God views us, as— for that matter—hopefully we view our own children. This applies, not only or even primarily to our brethren within the church, but to men *qua* men. That is perhaps the critical difference between Good News and bad news."

In the summer of 1964 Jon participated in a clinical-training program at Willard State Hospital, Willard, New York, under the direction of the Rev. Edward Tulis. This, too, proved to be an important experience for him, in which he learned more about working with people and about himself.

The problems with which Jon was wrestling in terms of Christian growth and development, and the way in which he was beginning to see them, were set forth in a letter to a fellow student in the fall of 1964: "I am trying to look appreciatively yet critically at our common 'life in the Spirit.' . . . I think sometimes we are afraid to admit that our religion is anything other than a (rather precarious) intellectual venture. I think I know why—but I can testify with assurance that the causes are not invincible. If we dare not suspend our critical activities *here* to confess and explore the lonely, glorious absurdity of our life in Christ, we shall have a difficult time being faithful shepherds. . . ."

Concerning the Church he told his friend, Carlton Russell: "The Church still needs priests and prophets, men who through word and sacrament will wage the sword of peace, who will proclaim with the totality of their lives that the way of the Cross is ultimately the road of life and that the ongoing sacrifice of the Cross is the only triumph of significant value. You will find again and again, as you have already found, that it is almost easier to preach it than to live it. But you will also find, when you have fallen as low as a man can fall and the whole bloody business is going down the plug-o, that what you need is yours for the asking. I know this only too well. You may lose your faith (as I have for a time several times), and still the One Who calls you in love will not let you go unless you freely choose. The risk is great—but so is the joy."

How difficult the path of development could be came strikingly to Jon's attention in a class discussion on a paper that he had written on the doctrines of Atonement and Holy Spirit. In the course of the discussion, Jon was asked for definitions of some of the terms he had used. His immediate reaction was harsh and negative; he did not wish to play "word games." As participants continued to press Jon, his replies were less than generous. When the discussion ended, everyone left angry and frustrated. Apologies were soon made, and out of the controversy several friendships developed. But the incident did demonstrate that Jon could be a rigid and opinionated young man, prepared to override the feelings of others to maintain his point. In commenting later about the discussion, the professor present made this evaluation: "Perhaps of more importance than the content of his presentation was his attitude. There was a pedantic air about his presentation that conveyed an aloofness, or a self-conscious superiority, or a developed conviction on the subject that would tolerate only with impatience any fundamental challenge."

The Call to Selma

In March, 1965, Dr. Martin Luther King, Jr., issued his urgent call to all men of good will to support with their physical presence the crucial civil rights struggle fast developing to a climax in Selma, Alabama. That call and the events that were to ensue at Selma were to alter radically the course of Jon's life—and to precipitate his death.

Dr. King's call reached the students at ETS in the early evening of March 10. It appealed to their sense of social justice, and a number immediately responded. The questions "Are you going?"

and "Are you coming with us?" were repeatedly asked as students passed one another in the halls or visited in the dormitories. Jon himself put the latter question to Judith Upham, a fellow student (and a 1964 graduate of Radcliffe College). Judy had not quite decided, but Jon's urgent asking of the question evoked the response, "Yes, well I guess so. How are we going?" A few hours later, having checked everything out with parents and the school, the Boston contingent, including Jon and Judy, was on its way to Selma via Atlanta.

When the plane landed in Atlanta, the students went directly to the office of the Southern Christian Leadership Conference, where —in fact, in Dr. King's office—they spent the night. No one got much sleep, but then they had not traveled all those miles for that. Instead, they talked and laughed and prayed together. In the morning they boarded buses for the remainder of the journey to Selma. As they drove, instruction was given in the techniques of nonviolent demonstration, and the remainder of the time was spent singing freedom songs, in discussion, and occasionally resting for a few minutes.

On arrival in Selma, the bus driver, unhappy in the first place about transporting the group, sought directions. He pulled into a street that appeared to be the right one but the police would not allow him to stop. He thereupon drove the group about one and one-half miles from the town's center and dropped them off in a big field; from there the group trudged back to town, passing on the way groups of white people, sitting on their porches, who glared at them. It was a rather traumatic introduction to Selma, and the group appreciated Jon's good humor and sensitivity to the situation.

On arrival in the Negro district of Selma, the students joined the assembly of demonstrators from all parts of the country, but owing to the considerable confusion that prevailed, they soon found that it would be impossible for them to stay together as an ETS group. Many of these demonstrators were simply wandering about the district in the hope of learning when the march to Montgomery would begin. This had been their reason for coming to Selma.

No one, however, was to march to Montgomery for many days. Attempts, to be sure, were made—impressive attempts led by Dr.

King, with hundreds of people, linked arm in arm, singing freedom songs as they marched down the streets of Selma to the
bridge that led toward Montgomery. At the bridge they were
stopped and turned back by massed lines of armed police.

Jon participated in these attempts and, like the other demonstrators, felt the frustration and exhaustion that accompanied these
marching maneuvers. In recalling those feelings, Judy Upham
put it this way: "Most of us felt double-crossed. Here we had
come all the way from Cambridge prepared to march to Montgomery, and they only let us walk across the bridge. So we all
marched up, clear up to the line of troopers. They marched the
whole line up that far and then turned it around, and had lines
going both ways for awhile, and marched back. We stood around
exhausted. We hadn't really walked that far, but then we hadn't
gotten much sleep the night before."

By nightfall some demonstrators, including a number of the
ETS group who had pressing student obligations back in Cambridge, decided to leave Selma. Others, including Jon and Judy,
decided to stay and found accommodations for themselves in
Negro homes in the George Washington Carver Project. Thus
Jon put down his first roots in Selma and in the "movement."
Meanwhile, mass meetings were being held almost continuously
at Brown's Chapel. The Rev. James J. Reeb, of Boston, had
been beaten and killed in the open. If danger had been remote in
their minds up to that point, it now took on for the demonstrators
an immediate and more realistic dimension.

The following morning (March 12), a march on the courthouse was called to protest the killing of James Reeb. The police,
however, had closed off that route, and most of the marchers—
that is, the many clergy who had come from their distant parishes
to join the protest for a day or two—refused to attempt to break
the police lines. Because of this refusal the leadership were unable
to carry out the planned march. Frustration then began to be
the mood of the protesters. It soon turned itself, however, into a
new determination. A second attempt to march on the courthouse
also failed because by that time the police had both ends of the
street blocked off. Of what happened next, Judy gives this on-
the-scene report: "Sometime in the middle of the afternoon, after
another march attempt that didn't get very far at all, because by

now the police had both ends of the street very nicely blocked off, we decided to have a street vigil. 'By golly, we're marching, and if you won't let us march, we're going to stand here until we do.' The whole street practically all the way down was lined with marchers five abreast. We kept saying, 'We're going to march, we're going to march.' We never did. We kept standing around. Finally it became, 'We're not going to march, but we're not going to leave.' So we started this street vigil." As night came on, blankets, coffee, and sandwiches were provided by residents of the housing project.

For Jon and Judy, new to the movement, the painful and painstaking slowness of accomplishment in anything having to do with racial equality was becoming clear. When, at one point, the line moved some twenty yards up the street before being stopped, Jon commented, "This symbolizes the progress of the Negro race in the last hundred years. You stand around and wait and then you move forward an inch or two."

Jon and Judy had now to ask themselves whether they should return to Cambridge or remain longer in Selma. Jon talked about it with Priscilla Dolloff, another member of the Boston group, who suggested that he count the white faces still in line. Jon looked and counted, and in a second or two, he came back and announced that he would stay. Judy agreed to do the same: they would remain in Selma perhaps until Saturday, then return to Cambridge in time for their Sunday assignments.

That night they were invited to have dinner with some new-found friends, without realizing that they were expected by the family with whom Jon had spent the preceding night. There were some hurt feelings, and, as Judy now explains: "We were becoming more and more aware of the kinds of things you have to watch out for, particularly with regard to people's feelings. You have to be careful not to hurt, and how you manage to live in six places at once when one person thinks you're living exclusively with them is no mean accomplishment."

After supper they watched the police secure the barricades to keep the "outsiders" out and the "insiders" in. They also learned that evening something that was to cause another postponement of their leaving, planned for the following day, Saturday. They learned that on Wednesday some members of the Episcopal

Church who were in Selma for the protest had approached the rector of the local Episcopal parish about their plan to attend worship on Sunday as an integrated group. They were received politely, and the rector explained that it was the ushers' responsibility to decide who would be admitted to services. (The canon law of the Episcopal Church reads differently.) He could not tell them at this time who the ushers would be, and he made no effort to find out. He also gave it as his opinion that the problem would be more happily settled if everyone went back to their homes and left the local church undisturbed.

On Saturday Jon and Judy decided to join the others in their decision to test the situation on Sunday and, accordingly, deferred their return to Cambridge. On Sunday the integrated group sought to attend the 11 o'clock service. They were met at the church door by the ushers, who refused them admittance. Malcolm E. Peabody, of Boston, former national president of the Episcopal Society for Cultural and Racial Unity (ESCRU), attempted without success to reason with the ushers. The group then conducted a service of Morning Prayer on the sidewalk in front of the church.

On Monday (March 14) permission to march on the courthouse was secured, and the march, an impressive affair, took place the same afternoon. The demonstrators marched two by two about ten feet apart, according to Judy Upham's recollection; lining the streets were all sorts of white people, some with shotguns and rifles. But there were no incidents.

Jon and Judy had supper that evening with the family who were housing Jon in the project. During supper the teenagers of the family returned home excited that an important Selma official shook hands with them when they had thanked him for protecting the marchers. It appeared to Jon and Judy that what really astonished and amazed these youngsters was the fact that a white police official had accorded them the dignity of recognition. Judy put it this way: "For most of these kids, except for the outsiders, this was a first white someone who had ever done as dignified a thing as sort of treating them as people. It was the greatest thing to watch, and terrible because it was so new to them, something they never expected, yet a common incident in most white people's lives."

That night President Johnson delivered his historic civil rights address to Congress. Everyone in Selma participating in the protest was jubilant, yet some, including Jon, wondered what they and the others had accomplished by marching on the courthouse, and whether anything that meant real permanent change had been achieved. So far as they could see, the fact that it had taken from Wednesday to the following Monday to do no more than march on the courthouse was indeed discouraging, and more astonishing still was the fact that such a thing should happen at all.

Jon and Judy now planned to leave Selma Tuesday afternoon—they were not contemplating any return—and would have done so had they not missed the bus to Montgomery. It was purely accidental: just prior to departure time Jon found that he was without cigarettes and went to a nearby store to buy a pack; by the time he returned, the bus had left, and their departure was again postponed one more day. They returned to their "project" friends for housing and spent the evening with them, hearing about what life in the Selma Negro ghetto was like when there were no demonstrations to divert the attention of the police. Into the late hours of the night story after story was told, all similar in their accounts of white terror and threats.

After their friends had finished their stories and gone to bed, Jon, Judy, and Morris Samuels, an Episcopal minister who had joined them earlier, sat up and talked together about the meaning of what they had heard. They asked themselves the question, What will happen to these people after the demonstrators leave? All three were upset by what they guessed would happen. Morris Samuels recalls remarking to Jon: "I am terribly concerned for this 'wham-bam-thank-you-ma'am' ministry of Selma when hundreds of clergymen sort of explode into town and then kind of make it on a Friday night so they can get back on Sunday to preach their sermons." Just before retiring Morris Samuels made an observation that was to influence greatly Jon Daniels' life: "Well, you know I can't really tell you what to do. But if I were in that position, the one thing I would ask is 'How dare I leave now?'" In retrospect, however, Morris Samuels has also said this about the experience: "I think it would be fair to say that Jon was a naïve young seminarian as I was a naïve young priest in the movement. We had many idealistic notions. But certainly, as we shared our concerns and our experiences, the one thing that came to ring true to us was that our major common bond was our concern for the relevancy of the faith and the relevancy of the church."

For an hour and a half afterward Jon and Judy continued to analyze the situation. If they were to return to Selma, they asked themselves, was there anything they could do? Perhaps help with voter registration or assist teenagers with school problems? What would their return mean in relation to their studies? So far as their studies went, both felt that they could manage their academic obligations whether in Selma or in Cambridge. They finally concluded that their major problem would be to obtain permission to carry on their studies in Selma. Jon knew that his mother would not be pleased but would accept his decision. Judy thought that her parents would respond in the same way. They were not sure about the ETS faculty.

The next day, Wednesday, they returned to Cambridge and immediately presented their proposal to Acting Dean Henry M. Shires, who questioned them about it. Because they were so clear and thoughtful and determined about returning to Selma, he felt that they were probably right. He spoke to them of the action of the Holy Spirit and the power of the Spirit to move in the lives of men and women. The next day the faculty gave official approval. Meanwhile, the Rev. John Morris, executive director of ESCRU, agreed that his organization would sponsor their return.

Return to Selma

When Jon and Judy arrived in Selma the great march to Montgomery was just moving out across the bridge. They did not leave Selma with the marchers, but spent the next two days there settling in. Then they joined the marchers for the final five-mile stretch into Montgomery. On reaching Montgomery, all the marchers were jubilant. Jon, too, was joyous, almost buoyant, as well as grateful to be back.

Late that afternoon, after the march, thousands of demonstrators were seeking transportation home. Jon and Judy drove a group of teenagers back to Selma. On arrival at Selma they were asked to return to Montgomery and pick up others who needed transportation. Since they had a Volkswagen with Massachusetts license plates, they refused. They were conscious of the danger and unwilling to risk it. That same night Viola Gregg Liuzzo, a civil rights worker from Detroit, was murdered while transporting Negroes who had been in the Montgomery march.

The next few weeks Jon and Judy devoted to an attempt to integrate St. Paul's Episcopal Church, Selma, meeting frequently with the Rev. T. Frank Mathews, Jr., rector of St. Paul's, to discuss the matter. But each Sunday morning they would arrive at the church only to be met with hostile stares and occasionally impolite remarks from parishioners. During the week they would again discuss the situation with Mr. Mathews in the privacy of his office in an attempt to ameliorate the situation, but nothing came of those discussions.

Mr. Mathews then requested the group to refrain from attending services as an integrated group on Easter Sunday. This was agreed, since Mr. Mathews did indicate some intention to ease the situation. They found later, however, that some Negro young people planned to attend Easter Sunday Services at St. Paul's. Jon and Judy felt they could not let the young people go by themselves, and decided to see Mathews once again. They explained the problem to him, and their intention to attend only the 7:30 service. Jon was preaching elsewhere at 11 o'clock. Mr. Mathews continued to feel that they were intruding upon the Selma congregation and that they should be back at the seminary.

As they left the church, Jon was stopped by a man who asked if he were trying to wreck the church. When Jon, in the course of his reply, answered, "We're trying to live the gospel," the man looked at him, and said, "Go to hell, you ———," and continued with other vituperative remarks. This attack typified the treatment they received from some members of St. Paul's. There were a few, a very few, people in the parish who tried to be nice, and who were helpful, but on the whole the situation was most discouraging.

Easter Sunday Jon and Judy joined the five young people who planned to attend the early service at St. Paul's. Judy recalls: "As we approached the church, the head usher pulled Jon aside and asked him not to bring anyone to the eleven o'clock service. Jon told him quietly that he was preaching at a Negro church at eleven and that there was no need to worry."

The ushers made no effort to welcome the group into the church. They seated them in the last row in the side aisle section, although there were at least six empty pews in front of them. A wooden partition between the two halves of the pew allowed the group no opportunity to spread out. To Judy it seemed that the ushers were making absolutely sure that everybody else would be communicated and back in their seats before she and Jon and the others would be allowed to receive Communion.

This incident led the Episcopal Society for Cultural and Racial Unity, under whose sponsorship Jon and Judy had come to Selma, to issue a statement which read in part: "A new form of segregation is emerging in the Episcopal Diocese of Alabama where the Bishop has indicated that ushers at Episcopal parishes may seat visitors, including Negroes and integrated groups, at their discretion. On Easter Sunday, in Selma at St. Paul's Church such a group was made to sit in the rear because the service was to be a celebration of the Holy Communion. They were the last allowed to receive the Sacrament. In the face of Church canon law, adopted last fall and requiring that persons be admitted to Episcopal churches without regard to color, it now appears that insidious devices will be employed to circumvent the spirit of the canon and the generally accepted teaching of the Church. Ironically, in the state where seating-from-the-rear on buses was first challenged, the Church now seeks to use the nefarious method of segregated seating to maintain the old racial patterns. That such separation may be required only at services where there is to be Holy Communion only intensifies the affront to Christ and His Church. . . ."

In a separate letter to Bishop Carpenter, Jon Daniels and Judy Upham wrote on April 28: "The issue is the objective fact of the policy of racial discrimination practiced by St. Paul's, Selma and endorsed yesterday by the Diocesan of Alabama. Please remember, Sir, that the seating policy of St. Paul's, *as it applies specifically to us,* has been explicitly announced to us by the rector of that parish as being discriminating in purpose. . . . Therefore we cannot accede to your insistence that we 'go to Church with eyes closed and just worship the Lord without looking for faults.' The terms of the canon and the teachings of the Church force us to regard as irrelevant in the present case your insistence that we wait humbly and thankfully for our turn at the Lord's table. . . . Genuine humility implies for us, as white Christians, steadfast refusal to accept any violation of either the letter or the spirit of this canon. There is a difference between humility and humiliation."

It is interesting in the context of this letter to reflect upon an incident that occurred at ETS only one month earlier. The faculty had voted to request that the Executive Council of the Episcopal Church reconsider a vote it had taken that denied certain monies to clergymen who worked in dioceses of the Episcopal Church without the permission of the bishop of that diocese. The issue came before a meeting of the students' governmental organization known as the St. John's Society. At that meeting Jon argued in favor of the Executive Council's position, claiming that the Episcopal Church is, by definition, a church governed by bishops and to vote against the Executive Council was to deny the very foundation of the Church's polity. Once such a precedent was set, who could know where it might lead? The whole structure of the Church might eventually crumble. Following his well-argued and fascinating plea to refrain from censuring the Executive Council, Jonathan sat down to the boos of his fellow seminarians.

It is a measure of the impact of Selma on Jon that only a few weeks later, certainly without the permission of the bishop of that diocese, he was to challenge the position of the bishop with respect to the issue of integration at St. Paul's, Selma.

Jon and Judy were also involved at about the same time in a demonstration in Camden, Alabama, where they encountered tear gas for the first time. Other than the Selma vigil and the Montgomery march, this was the only major demonstration they participated in during their stay in Alabama. For the most part, their return stay in Alabama was uneventful. Occasionally they were followed, and once they found it necessary to move to another home because threats were made on the family with whom they were staying.

Jon frequently attended St. Elizabeth's Roman Catholic Church (after attending Episcopal services), because he felt accepted by the community there. In fact, he came to consider Father Maurice Ouellet, the pastor, his spiritual adviser while he was in Selma. "It was really quite natural that Jon Daniels should come and worship with us," Father Ouellet later declared. "After all, he was living in the Negro section of town with a Negro family. The white community was not the community in which he was really living down here. That is one of the reasons why there was little joy for him in worship at St. Paul's Church, and why he felt alien there. He went out of loyalty, I think, and out of a desire to help fuse the two communities; yet he was aware of the fact that such fusion wasn't very close to accomplishment. So he did feel that this was his church, that he could come here and worship and be part of this Christian community. And I was rather proud at the time that Jon would say that even though he himself was not a Roman Catholic, he considered me his pastor. It was a nice touch, part of that gentle touch that he had."

On many occasions Jon was called a "white nigger." He recalled such an incident in his essay, "A Burning Bush." He knew that those who so branded him did it maliciously, but the label did not particularly displease him. He had, after all, gone South in order to identify with the Negro, to participate fully in the life of the Negro. Ironically, for Jon there was something positive in the expression "white nigger." It meant that he was making his point, that he was indeed being seen at least by white men as a brother of those with whom he now lived. He did not, however, comprehend the depth of hatred seething beneath the epithet. Though a man of strong feelings himself, Jon never really understood such all-consuming hate. He simply could not believe it.

Father Ouellet, probably more than any other person, tried to warn Jon of the danger to which he was open by his intimate involvement with the movement in Alabama. Jon would talk about this danger and even the possibility of his own death, yet Father Ouellet sensed that Jon did not really believe anything would actually happen to him. Jon just did not sufficiently comprehend that he was already a likely target for rabid segregationists.

Father Ouellet, who himself had faced death for his commitment, determined to make the issue clear to "his parishioner." In the course of a conversation, when Jon reported that he and Judy had on their previous trip stopped at a roadstand and acknowledged to the attendants their participation in the civil rights movement, Ouellet cautioned, " 'Jon, you just don't do things like that. They could have left the two of you for dead.' Jon looked at me with a puzzled expression on his face," Ouellet recalls, "as if he found my words strange. I was telling him something new when I said this. I was trying to tell him, 'You don't have to do this kind of thing. Keep going, man. Stay out of those places, especially if Judy is with you. They're looking for people like you.' " Those words, it seemed to Father Ouellet, hit the mark, and Jon's future actions were to reflect a new consciousness of the danger that he was in.

Spring Interlude

In May, Jon returned to ETS and plunged immediately into preparation for his final examination and the writing of a term paper.

When these tasks were completed, he did much soul-searching and spoke to many friends, including the writer, about his impending return to begin earnest work in the Deep South. He did not receive support and encouragement from everyone as, on the whole, he had when he made his earlier decision to return to Selma. It was the writer's opinion that since, by Jon's own admission his studies had suffered, he should take the summer to rest up, refresh himself, catch up some of his course work, perhaps do some writing, then return to ETS and make the most of his senior year. After that, if he so decided, he could return to his Selma ministry. Jon was not convinced. He did, however, weigh the matter with other friends. The following day he announced his firm decision to return: "I have promises to keep. I told my friends in Selma that I would be back soon. They trust me. If I don't return this summer, why should they ever trust any white man again?"

In this same conversation, we discussed the situation in Alabama and the death which might soon be his. He seemed aware that this was a real possibility and that it might actually happen to him, although, as often with men in the front line, there may have been a deep-down disbelief that death would come to him. As he left, his last words were, "Well, I may get killed, but if I do, it won't be because I was careless."

During the early summer following successful completion of his exams at ETS, Jon attended, as a member of the senior staff, the Diocesan Youth Conference in his home state of New Hampshire. He was asked to submit a "piece" for the conference daily paper, and complied with a short article entitled "Magnificat in a Minor Key."

" 'He hath filled the hungry with good things; and the rich he hath sent empty away.' So the lyric of radical upheaval, of social and political and economic revolution, the world-breaking, world-shaping utterance of Amos and his heirs echo in Mary's glad song. Her Son was a son of the poor. He got the treatment the poor have usually gotten.

"So we, too, set our faces to go to Jerusalem, the holy city, as He has gone before us . . . to preach good news to the poor . . . to proclaim release to the captives, and recovering of sight to the blind, to set at liberty those who are oppressed, to proclaim the acceptable year of the Lord. Like Him we seek Jerusalem 'not to destroy men's lives, but to save them.' We go to make our witness to the Truth that has set us free. We go to stand in (often silent) compassion with the captives and the blind and the oppressed. We go not so much to 'comfort' as to love and to heal and to free. Our motives must be loving and our methods chaste. . . . One begins by listening—making sure that one is really *listening*. Then there is the quiet matter of rolling up one's sleeves. . . ."

During these months there was also an opportunity to visit with his mother and grandparents and to renew hometown friendships. Mrs. Daniels, after Dr. Daniels' death, had resumed teaching French in a public high school. It had not been easy during the winter months, therefore, to find time for much visiting, and these few days together were anticipated with real joy by both mother and son, though Mrs. Daniels was troubled, knowing that Jon would soon be leaving once again for Selma. She was resigned, however, to his decision.

She knew there was nothing she could do to persuade him otherwise. Many others had tried. Further, she knew that she could not deny him what he believed he must do. By now Jon had a profound sense of "call." He was not in his own mind returning simply because he wanted to return—he had no choice. When a friend asked him why he had to go back South, he responded, "It's going to come sometime and it has to start somewhere."

The family coveted those summer days of 1965 with Jon at home. His Grandmother Weaver recalls that on his way to Geneva Point, Jon stopped to visit in Meredith, New Hampshire: "That visit does mean so much to all of us. We had good talks at the table many times. There were of course many things that I had in mind to talk further with him about. . . ."

We should pause here to make note of Jon's theology as it reflected itself in his discussions and particularly in his essays. One professor observed with reference to Jon's discussions: "Jon was not one to hesitate to speak about his faith in sure confidence that in some way words and truth are intimately related even if we do not always know in just what way that may be. His Easter conversion experience a couple of years earlier had rooted him too firmly in God for doubt seriously any longer to be a problem."

Last Mission to Alabama

When the time for the journey back to Selma arrived, Jon was ready—in fact, anxious—to return to his Selma friends, and the work that he believed was his to do. His objectives were to cultivate the friendships he already had established in the "Negro community," to establish better relations, if possible, with members of the "white community," perhaps to act as a bridge between the two, and to keep integrated St. Paul's Church—a project for which he felt a special responsibility. He did not return to Selma primarily to demonstrate; yet if that were necessary, he would no doubt do so.

One specific task Jon hoped to achieve was to prepare and distribute information about welfare and other community services available to residents of the Negro ghetto. As a representative of the Episcopal Society for Cultural and Racial Unity, Jon collaborated with Eugene Pritchett of the Student Nonviolent Coordinating Committee (SNCC) in the publication of a *Memorandum to Dallas County Residents in Need of Public Assistance*. This was a listing and brief description of the county, state, and federal agencies and other resources technically available to those in need of some form of assistance.

The memorandum closed with the words: "By taking advantage of the resources that are available to you, you can improve the life, health, and well-being of your family—and of the entire community. It's up to you. Good luck." What had seemed at first a fairly easy task turned, in fact, into a major undertaking. Extensive investigation was necessary to ensure the accuracy of the information reported. On July 30, 1965, the memorandum was ready for distribution, and Jon then turned to assisting with voter registration in Lowndes County.

Lowndes County, Alabama, was then, and remains, one of the most fully segregated areas of the South. Until March, 1965, although over eighty percent of the population were Negroes, there were no registered Negro voters in the county. With an active Ku Klux Klan and a frightened Negro citizenry, the movement for civil rights, which by this time had made some impact in most places in Alabama, had hardly been heard of here. Federal voting registrars were finally sent in to Lowndes County, and SNCC undertook to encourage and assist Negroes to register to vote.

How difficult a task this turned out to be for those working on the assignment, including Jon, Stokely Carmichael later made clear in a talk to the students at ETS: "When I started working in the Movement I used to say to people, 'If you get out and vote you will get a decent school, you'll get more money.' I really believed that. I believed it because it had been told to me when I was in school. In the morning when I get up and I walk around

Lowndes County and I see Mrs. ———, she says, 'Stokely, you told me if I voted my children would go to better schools, and get better jobs and that we would have some justice in the South.' I say, 'Yes, Ma'am.' And she says, 'Well, my boss man just told me to leave because I voted. Now you find me a house and a job.' That's the problem I have to face every day. Fifty families have been displaced in Lowndes County. They have doubled up with other families; some of them live in tents. Every day I have to meet people who ask me, 'Where am I going to go?' These are the questions I have to face." Though voting might not solve the specific problems immediately, it could eventually become an effective weapon in the fight for equal rights for all citizens. There was a general feeling that something had to be done to overcome the fears and hesitancy of the people.

Talking specifically about Jon and his work, Stokely Carmichael said: "Jon was known in Lowndes County for a number of reasons. Number one, unlike many other ministers who came to Alabama he didn't spend his time talking to ministers. He spent his time talking to the people in Lowndes County, so that they knew him, and he knew them. He, as a matter of fact, knew very few ministers at all in Alabama, but he knew the people. . . . Willie started working with Jon about two weeks after Jon was in the county. And he started to get strength from Jon. He started to develop his own internal strength. That is something that Jon Daniels had and I think everybody strives for. He had an abundance of strength that came from the inside that he could give to people and that he did give to people. The people in Lowndes County realized that with the strength they got from Jon Daniels they had to carry on, they had to carry on!"

On August 12, Jon was present at a meeting in Birmingham of the Southern Christian Leadership Conference (SCLC). He had high respect for Dr. Martin Luther King and in every way wanted to assist him in his efforts.

At the meeting Jon met the Rev. Richard Morrisroe, a young Roman Catholic priest from St. Columbanus Church, Chicago. Father Richard, as he was called, had been active in protests against *de facto* school segregation in Chicago. Wanting to know and to understand his Negro parishioners better, he had come to

Alabama to learn what he could firsthand about their backgrounds.

Thursday night Jon and Father Richard drove to Selma. Jon was anxious to get back to work. He had told a friend in Birmingham that "he was tired of talk and he felt he was doing something about it, something so basic as preparing and distributing a list of welfare aids and services for people long accustomed to being the stepchildren of society."

Arrest in Fort Deposit

On Friday Jon and Father Richard went to Lowndes County to be on hand for a demonstration scheduled there for Saturday. They were joined by Gloria Larry and Willie Vaughn, two Negroes working for SNCC in Fort Deposit, the town in which the demonstration was to take place. Early Saturday they drove to Fort Deposit.

Jon was certainly aware of the danger he and others faced. He had, while driving, been shot at on more than one occasion. "I can always outrun a bullet," he remarked, and he was driving a new rented Plymouth Fury with precisely that in mind. The cautions that he was taking would indicate that he was in no way attempting to provoke the violent act that would cause his death a week later.

On arriving in Fort Deposit, Jon did not intend to demonstrate, but only to advise, to assist, and to take some photographs. The demonstration was to be a march on and picketing of Herb's City Cafe, McGrough's grocery store, and Waters' drygoods store. It had been planned by local young people, in the hope of encouraging their elders to become actively involved in seeking their rights.

Jon arrived with Father Morrisroe, Stokely Carmichael, and three or four other SNCC workers around 9:30 A.M. They immediately joined the local leaders and David Gordon to talk over the plans for the demonstration. "The problem of the moment," as David Gordon later recalled, "was whether the Fort Deposit teenagers who were to join the demonstration would remain nonviolent when struck or beaten during the arrests that all assumed would take place. The SNCC leadership was wavering between a decision to ask that the demonstration be called off if the teenagers refused to practice nonviolence and a recommendation to just try to convince the youngsters to be nonviolent and letting them go ahead." The group finally decided that it was not SNCC's business to issue orders but to act in a purely advisory capacity. They decided to do all they could to encourage nonviolence but not to insist upon it. There was, in any case, little else they could do. Jon agreed with these decisions.

Jimmie Rogers, who at this time was living in Fort Deposit, was the leader of the demonstration. In preliminary conversation with Jimmie, Jon specifically indicated that he did not intend personally to participate in the demonstration. Shortly thereafter, however, Jon realized that most of the SNCC workers were not going to take part because there were not many of them and they wanted to stay out of jail in order to continue working in Lowndes County. When Jon saw the group of teenage marchers, pathetically few in number and frightened by what they knew was about to happen, he decided that he must join them to offer his moral support.

For the young people in the group this was to be their first demonstration. Jon, on the other hand, was a seasoned marcher. After a lengthy discussion about nonviolence, at 11:30 A.M., the demonstrators began the walk into town. They were to be arrested by the local police "for their own protection," and had been so informed by an agent of the Department of Justice.

The demonstrators divided into three groups in order to approach the downtown blocks from three different directions. Jon was in a group of about ten marchers who went downtown along a side street. David Gordon recalls: "As they passed by near where we were waiting, Jon was talking to the younger kids. It seemed as though he were trying to prop them up. And he was joking and smiling as he always was in situations like this. He looked very calm. He had been in a very joking mood earlier when we were talking. I remember that at that time I was impressed by the difference between Jon and Father Morrisroe. Father Morrisroe was much more reserved, in part I think because he was such a recent arrival and hadn't gotten used to the situation. Jon was almost a veteran by then."

The group to which Jon was assigned managed to get downtown and to walk along the sidewalk in front of the target stores. They carried signs protesting the indignities that Negroes had suffered at the hands of whites in that community.

It has been reported, although there is uncertainty about it, that the group was at this point placed under arrest by Fort Deposit's one Negro policeman. They were taken, in any event, firmly but quietly to the town jail. The other demonstrators had meanwhile been taken into custody before reaching downtown. All groups were arrested at about 11:45 A.M. Jon asked a policeman if he was not infringing upon the demonstrators' constitutional rights. He was told that the demonstrators had no constitutional rights in Fort Deposit.

Since it was a Saturday morning, everyone was out to observe Fort Deposit's first demonstration, an incredible sight both to whites and Negroes—incredible to the whites because they could not believe "their" Negroes would take a public stand in opposition to them, and to the Negroes because they could not believe that among them were some who would risk home, job, arrest, and perhaps life by taking part in such a demonstration.

Negro onlookers stood on one side of the downtown block, frightened and concerned about what was happening. The whites, edgy and belligerent, stood on a street perpendicular to that from which the Negroes watched.

David Gordon describes the scene: "We'd been going back and forth on that block all morning. The local whites had labeled the whites in the demonstration 'freedom riders'—to them still a threatening term, although it had been in disuse elsewhere for a long time. All along that block, white men had been threatening us and telling us to get out of town. This is the side of the block along which the group of protesters which Jon joined was walking when arrested and taken off to jail. By the time they were arrested the cluster of whites was really large. A number of white citizens, who had apparently been temporarily appointed deputies marched along with the police and county officials as they escorted the demonstrators to jail. A lot of them had clubs and many of them had rifles—shotguns mainly. We didn't hear any of the comments that were made to the demonstrators by the white people because we were keeping our distance. They marched their prisoners across the tracks, and all three groups, now combined, were put in a small dollhouse structure probably no more than ten by fifteen feet."

For about twenty minutes the prisoners were confined in this cramped Fort Deposit jail, before the police began to process them. Their names were taken and they were searched for weapons. A garbage truck was driven up to the jail, and one by one they were ordered into the back, where garbage would ordinarily be dumped.

Meanwhile, many whites had gathered around the jail, and some were giving orders about the loading operation. Negroes had also gathered, but on the other side of the railroad track. It was clear they were to stay on that side, whereas the whites had freedom to come and go any place they liked. The Negroes wanted to help their friends but, in fact, there was nothing that they could do.

When a group of reporters who had not participated in the demonstration drove up to the jail in a car with a broken window, the crowd turned their attention on them. At first, they were simply curious about how the car window had been broken. But their mood quickly changed to one of hostility, one man fanning their anger with a hysterical speech.

When the garbage truck finally drove off, "the prisoners on it," David Gordon reports, "began to sing and pointedly waved to the Negroes across the tracks in a gesture of reassurance. Jon himself appeared calm, singing and waving with the others."

At Hayneville the prisoners were put in a jail almost as wretched as the one in Fort Deposit—stopped toilets, no bathing facilities, poor food. They were housed in three cells; Jon was in a cell with Stokely Carmichael and Chris Wildy among others. At first, they were denied visitors, but later several friends were admitted, and on these occasions they had a brief opportunity to review their situation. Bail for each had been set at $100. The prisoners agreed among themselves, however, that all would remain in jail until enough money was raised to accomplish a general release. When Henri Stines of ESCRU arrived with bail money for Jon, Jon promptly refused to accept it.

The prisoners spent the six days and nights of their confinement talking, singing, reading, and holding services of worship. They ate what they were served, and got what rest they could.

Release in Hayneville

On Friday, to their mutual joy, the prisoners as a group were released on bail. Once outside the jail, the group sat on the lawn of the building to await transportation. Four local policemen ordered them off the property. They argued that it was federal property and that they were safer there than they would be walking around town. Again they were ordered to leave, and it was apparent that the policemen meant what they said. Willie Vaughn went to telephone for assistance, and the rest walked toward the corner.

Jon Daniels, Ruby Sales, Joyce Bailey, and Father Morrisroe walked together. When they arrived at the corner, Jon asked Ruby and Joyce whether they had money to buy soda pop for Father Morrisroe and himself. Ruby and Joyce told him yes, and the four headed down the street for a store which occupied a one-storied, peaked-roof structure painted a dull red with the usual Coca-Cola advertisement over the door, giving the name as "The Cash Store." Negroes shopped in this store because it was the only one in Hayneville that served them. Integrated groups of civil rights workers had been accepted there in the past. Jon, in fact, had been in the store previously, and that is no doubt why he suggested going there again. Certainly the group did not expect trouble as they approached the building. People could be seen shopping inside.

"When we got to the store," Ruby Sales recalls, "I was in front, and Jon, Joyce, and Father Morrisroe were behind me. And when we got to the door—I think I had walked up a step or two —this man, standing in the doorway with a shotgun, said, 'This store is closed.' Then, as I remember, this man Tom Coleman said, 'If you don't get off this god-damned property I'm going to blow your damned brains out. And I mean get off.' The next thing I knew someone pulled me from behind. I heard a shotgun blast and I looked and saw Jon falling. I lay down on the ground and then I heard another shotgun blast, and then I saw Father Morrisroe fall on the ground. And he lay there moaning for help —for somebody to help him—and he was just lying there moaning and moaning and moaning."

Joyce Bailey, shortly after the shooting, told the same story in her own words: "Actually I didn't see the man with the gun until we got to the door and he had the gun on Ruby, and Jon pushed Ruby to the ground. At that time the man shot Jon and Jon caught his stomach and fell. He didn't even say a word. So Father Richard caught me by the hand and jerked me around somebody's car. I don't know whose car it was. After Father Richard had done this, I started running and he ran with me. At this time this man shot Father Richard and I kept running. As I looked back Father Richard was falling to the ground and Ruby was on her knees crawling. Actually I thought the man had shot Ruby, and I turned around and helped Ruby get up. We ran across the street. . . ."

Jimmie Rogers, who was standing some distance away, reported: "I heard someone say, 'He has a gun, he has a gun.' Well, I didn't see who it was. So I looked up and down the street, and I saw Jon Daniels push Ruby Sales to the ground, and a man rush out with an automatic pump shotgun and he shot Jon and Jon fell down. . . ."

Richard Morrisroe from his bed in Oak Park Hospital, Chicago, repeated the story: "We were at the corner waiting. . . . Jimmie Rogers . . . went to arrange for transportation. We sat waiting for some time and then Jon said, 'Come on along, we'll go to the store.' . . . And I was coming along at the tail end of the group. . . . And I could see a figure in the door but I could hear more than I could see really. And the words were, 'Get the hell out of here or I'll blow your head off,' or something like that. I turned and started running really at this and heard one shot and then heard a second—the one that hit me."

For about half an hour confusion reigned. The others who had been released from jail scattered in search of protection. Finally, one or two ventured to examine Jon and Father Morrisroe.

Jon had been killed instantly by the first shotgun blast. Father Richard was out flat in the street, groaning for water. He was conscious and remained conscious until he underwent surgery at a hospital in Montgomery sometime later. In the meantime, Coleman, still brandishing his gun, warned off in a threatening way anyone who seemed ready to help the injured Morrisroe. A car approached and Coleman was driven off, taken to jail, and soon thereafter released on bail. Eventually, a local doctor and nurse arrived on the scene, and did what could be done to assist Father Morrisroe.

About three quarters of an hour after the shooting, Jon's body was taken to a funeral home. Word by this time had reached the SNCC office, and two doctors were immediately sent to the scene of the shooting. By the time the doctors arrived, however, the bodies had been removed, and no one present would say where they had been taken. SNCC workers, led by Shirley Walker, telephoned hospitals and funeral homes and ambulance services in Montgomery. No one knew anything. "No," they "hadn't picked up two bodies in Hayneville recently." They began calling hospitals, funeral homes, and ambulance services in Selma. The answers were the same. White's Chapel Funeral Home in Montgomery was called three times. They said that Jon's body was not at their home. St. Elizabeth's Hospital and St. Jude's Hospital, also in Montgomery, were contacted several times but claimed no knowledge of a wounded Roman Catholic priest named Morrisroe.

ESCRU was called in Atlanta and John Morris' intervention was asked. He repeated the Selma and Montgomery phone search with the same results. Shirley Walker, by this time desperate for word, called John Doar, Assistant Attorney General of the United States in charge of civil rights. She told him the situation, and asked him to help. About an hour later Doar returned the call saying he had located the two. Daniels' body was at White's Chapel Funeral Home in Montgomery. Father Morrisroe was in St. Elizabeth's Hospital, Montgomery.

Jon's Funeral

Friday, August 20, was Mrs. Daniels' birthday. When she checked her mailbox that morning and found no card from Jon, she thought it strange, since he never overlooked such occasions. But then she realized that he must be busy and so dismissed her concern and went about her tasks.

Her plans for the evening were to have dinner out with a close friend, Theresa Roberts, and later to join two other friends at Mrs. Roberts' home for a game of bridge. Just as the game started Mrs. Roberts' daughter called her on the telephone: "I just heard something awful . . . something about a Jon Daniels being killed . . . They said he was from New Haven." Mrs. Roberts assumed that it was another Jon Daniels, returned to the bridge table, and made no comment. When a second telephone message carried the same news, Mrs. Roberts asked that it be checked with the police. The report was confirmed, and Mrs. Roberts communicated the shocking news to Mrs. Daniels.

Frank Foley, the local funeral director and a friend of the Daniels' family, was asked to handle the funeral arrangements, the first step being to arrange the transportation of Jon's body from Montgomery to Keene. Ordinarily this would demand no more than routine attention. This case was different: air services from various airports refused to undertake the assignment. And although the initial attempt to make the arrangement was made at midnight on Friday, an air service was not engaged until Sunday at 6 P.M.; and it was John Morris who finally persuaded a Georgia friend to bring the body to Washington. From there he accompanied it to Keene.

During this period, Frank Foley recalls, "My telephone rang steadily. People were calling to ask, 'Is it true that this has happened?' The feeling of the local people was just beyond words. For everyone here who knew him, and for many who didn't, Jon's death cast a shadow that didn't begin to recede for a long time . . . for many people it never will."

On Monday and Tuesday mornings Jon's body lay in state at St. James' Episcopal Church, Keene. The news of his shocking death stirred the whole community, and persons from all walks of life and from many parts of the nation filed past his bier. The number was in the thousands.

The funeral service was held on Tuesday afternoon. Participating in the service were the former Presiding Bishop of the Episcopal Church, the Rt. Rev. Arthur Lichtenberger; the Rt. Rev. Charles F. Hall, Bishop of New Hampshire; the Very Rev. John B. Coburn, Dean of the Episcopal Theological School; the Rev. Dr. William J. Wolf, a member of the ETS faculty, and the Rev. Chandler H. McCarty, rector of St. James' Church, Keene.

In the congregation sat a delegation from Selma, including Ruby Sales, Willie Vaughn, Jimmie Rogers, and Stokely Carmichael. Mrs. Alonzo West, with whom Jon had lived in Selma, was also present, as well as Judy Upham and a delegation from ESCRU including Malcolm Peabody, John Morris, Kim Driesbach, and Malcolm Boyd.

In the service, hymns of victory were sung and the Holy Communion was celebrated. Professor Wolf read a paper which Jon had submitted as a class requirement not long before. Jon had written in part: "The faith with which I went to Selma has not *changed:* it has grown. Darkening coals have kindled. Faith has taken and flown with a song in its wings. 'My soul doth magnify the Lord, and my spirit hath rejoiced in God my Saviour. . . .' I lost fear in the black belt when I began to know in my bones and sinews that I had truly been baptized into the Lord's Death and Resurrection, that in the only sense that really matters I am already dead and my life is hid with Christ in God. . . ."

On Wednesday, August 25, a special service was held at the chapel of the Episcopal Theological School, at which Dean Coburn spoke. Other memorial services for Jonathan Daniels were held across the country in Protestant and Roman Catholic churches, and in Jewish synagogues. Memorable sermons were preached, that of the Rev. Daniel Berrigan, S.J., being among the noteworthy. Also, in his memory, there have been established a special book collection at VMI, and the Jonathan Myrick Daniels

Fellowship at the Episcopal Theological School. The latter, established by the Trustees, is to support the involvement of seminarians in areas of continuing social concern.

Following Jon's funeral by a few weeks and simultaneously with some of the memorial services, the last "official" drama was being acted out in Lowndes County. Coleman was duly indicted on a charge of manslaughter and a brief trial was held. Coleman's attorney argued that Jon Daniels had a knife in his hand and that Coleman feared for his life. The witnesses for the prosecution denied that Jon had any such weapon. The shooting occurred just after the group had been released from jail where they had been carefully searched both on entering and leaving. Jon, moreover, was committed to nonviolence. The jury heard these arguments, deliberated for one hour and forty-three minutes, and acquitted Coleman on the grounds that his action in shooting Jon Daniels was in self-defense. Thus concluded the official drama.

The press, however, in all parts of the country, including Alabama, deplored the jury's verdict. In a sharp statement the Presiding Bishop of the Episcopal Church, the Rt. Rev. John E. Hines, expressed well the indignation which was generally felt: "It is simply inconceivable to intimate acquaintances of both young men that Jonathan Daniels flashed a knife or that Father Morrisroe was armed. Alabama's own attorney general branded testimony that they were armed as perjury. The studied care with which the defense assassinated the character of a man already dead rightfully angers fair-minded men everywhere. The life of Jonathan Daniels is no more and no less valuable than that of any other man in the sight of God. But the cause in which he offered it is a cause dear to everyone who breathes the air of free men. Because of this free men must not permit the devastating verdict of the Hayneville twelve to be the final word of injustice in Alabama or anywhere else."

The Meaning of Jon Daniels' Obedience

The violence and the untimeliness of Jon's dying quite naturally focused attention on his life, caused many questions to be asked, particularly about his mission and commitment and about the meaning of his death.

Before considering these questions, however, it is well to remind ourselves that in its simplest terms and apart from the broader context Jon Daniels' death was the result of an act performed in behalf of the neighbor at his side. As he approached the Cash Store in Hayneville on that fatal day, he saw a man standing in the doorway with a gun. As the gun went up, he struck the young lady in front of him to the ground and took the bullet himself. In this sense he died simply because he saw someone in danger and responded to meet the need. Jon would have done this anywhere at any time for anyone, for he took seriously the command to love his neighbor, and he believed that there was a clear-cut connection between love of neighbor and one's willingness to die for him. With respect to his death, then, this much must everyone allow.

His death, however, also occurred in the context of the civil rights movement, and almost all the questions which it raised related to its meaning within that context.

It is no secret—nor unfaithfulness to him to note here—that Jon had qualms and doubts about his mission as well as strong convictions. These qualms and doubts he voiced on occasion to friends. For example, a fellow seminarian, Peter Selby, recalls Jon's questioning how long he should stay in Selma; what effect it would have on his seminary work; what direction should his ministry take; what about the attraction the Roman Catholic Church still had for him. But always, Selby recalls, Jon came back to the matter of obedience, obedience to God's call. This mattered above all else.

The writer also recalls that in several conversations Jon wondered whether his talents and energies and the effectiveness of his witness were best developed and employed in the work he was doing in Selma. Father Ouellet had a similar recollection and even went so far as to say, "Jon in a concrete way could not be very effective [on a permanent basis] in Selma. He was a stranger in a foreign land. He didn't fully understand the Negro really. He had just begun to grasp all this."

Like every man, then, Jon had his moments of confusion and

doubt, but, as Peter Selby reported, overriding these moments and shaping his life was his profound conviction of call and his determination to obey. The decisive role this conviction and determination played has been stated with great clarity by Professor Owen Thomas, of the Episcopal Theological School, when he answered the question, What was a New Hampshire boy doing in Alabama? in these words: "Jonathan Daniels did not go to Alabama in self-righteous anger, despising the white citizens of Selma, seeking for publicity and glory, hoping to do something dramatic like becoming a martyr. . . . He did not go to escape the subtler and more difficult problems of racial discrimination in Cambridge, Boston, or Keene, for he had been at work on those as well. He went sorrowfully and yet gladly, as a Christian man, who knew that he must stand with his brothers, both Negro and white, in their strife and suffering, to try to be a small channel for God's reconciling love in a country torn by hate and violence. He was not sure his presence would do any good. He was afraid that it might do some harm. He knew that his own motives were very mixed . . . that he was prejudiced, that at times he hated. He knew that all the things the white Southerners would say about him would have a grain of truth in them. He knew all this but he had to go. He had to go, because he believed deeply that being a Christian means more than believing the right things and being in favor of love and justice."

Jon Daniels "had to go" to Alabama. His final return to Selma was based on a short lifetime of decisions that made his last decision inevitable. To say "if only Jon had not returned" is to say "if only Jon had been another person"—but all who knew him would not have wanted him to be other than Jon Daniels.

LETTERS AND PAPERS

Autobiography I, 1957

Phantasmagoria

> *"All the world's a stage. And all the men and women merely players: they have their exits and their entrances; and one man in his time plays many parts, his acts being seven ages. . . ."*
>
> —WILLIAM SHAKESPEARE,
> in *As You Like It*

In etching this portrait of myself, I am trying, above all else, perhaps selfishly, to rediscover myself, to perceive clearly my personality and my nature, to find my course in "this trackless maze of lost stars." I am attempting to gaze with the eyes of my soul into the rippled, often troubled waters of my life, into the phantasmagoria of events and places, hopes and dreams, which is the symbolical reflection of my mortal existence; and there to find the secret, the essence of my life. Here I shall express my beliefs and ideals, that through thought, recognition, and expression of them, they may become strengthened and confirmed and that I may know their real value in and for my life. In here analyzing myself, I seek to recognize the influences that have thus far shaped the course of my life, and to meet both the external forces exerting pressure on me and the mysterious forces and fires which move and burn within me. Perhaps my goal, in reducing the equation to its simplest terms, lies deep in the valleys yet high amidst the stars, in the culmination of all these phases that is man's most profound question, age-old and eternal, "Whence came thou; whither goest thou?"

Born on March 20, 1939, in Keene, N.H., the first child of Dr. and Mrs. Philip Brock Daniels, I was christened Jonathan Myrick Daniels—a name which, to my later amusement, was taken from a Revolutionary War veteran ancestor's tombstone. Flowing apparently congenially through my American veins is the blood of a royal coachman who went to England with George I from Hanover and that of less haughty schoolteachers, fiery Gaelics, and gentle country doctors, a lieutenant in the Continental Army and a boy (my great-grandfather) who ran away from home to join, after lying about his age, the Union Army as a drummerboy in the Civil War, and who died on the West Coast during the Gold Rush. My first American ancestor, an Englishman bearing my first two names, settled in Massachusetts in the vicinity of what is now Lynn before the establishment of Plymouth Bay in 1620. I have dwelt in Keene for most of my life. However, when, during the war, my father went on maneuvers, we went with him, living in Washington, D.C., Pennsylvania, Kentucky, and Arkansas. Although I was only five at the time, I retain, with distinct clarity, more memories of that period than of any other time or place since. Despite the fact that now I cannot remember ideas long enough to put them on paper, I remember countless now cherished incidents that occurred during those years. I think of the South as my adopted home and because of this, I cannot help but sympathize with her—in fact I must confess that I have a great affection, I hope not too disloyal to my country and heritage, for the gallant and valorous but misguided Johnny Rebs.

Although I possess a reasonably good intellect and an above average potential, I have not particularly distinguished myself academically in the past several years. Until ninth grade I had straight A's and B's (and one C); then came my downfall. There I met a very charming young lady with whom I spent practically every waking moment, either in person or over the telephone. While this experience was excellent for my development as a young gentleman, it contributed less than nothing to my growth as a scholar, so that the following year I had a wretched time with the advanced Mathematics and Latin. When dawn finally arrived, belatedly, I found myself a trifle behind the eight ball, and, perhaps due to my inherent lackadaisical carelessness, I have never quite caught up.

My family and home have always been a great source of understanding and guidance, and I received at home, early, my first lessons of life along with training as a young but maturing gentleman. It was at home that, with my sister, of whom I am especially fond, I learned to get along with other people. Although there has existed for several years a considerable amount of tension and friction on the home front, this is no doubt not unusual, and it has not particularly influenced my outlook on life.

There are many influences both good and bad that have shaped the course of my life. The first of these, unconnected with my parents and home, was the books I read. Unlocking a great door to magnificent adventure, my books molded me into the type of person that I am when I was in the fourth grade. During that year, I fell prey to a complex of inferiority and jealousy that was to torment me for a period of six to seven years. This feeling of inferiority, combined with the normal emotional reactions of early adolescence, reached a climax in the ninth grade, where I was submerged in a long period of numerous black fits of depression (the Moods, as I used to call them), which nearly ruined my closest friendships and, at times, completely upset my equilibrium. I can never thank the young lady I mentioned before enough for her understanding patience and attempts to cheer me up. Although I spent far too much time with her, I learned a great deal from her and enjoyed with her a very fine friendship in which I learned, for one thing, how to put what I knew about being a gentleman into practice and, very simply, how to act with a member of the opposite sex.

In [that same fourth-grade] class, there were several boys, now leading athletes in school, who even then evidenced unusual athletic prowess. These classmates formed the sinecure of a small closed clique which has since evolved into the upper stratum of Keene High School student society—to which I was not able to gain admittance and to this day have not. For some reason, this now seemingly trivial failure inflicted a deep wound, the scar of which has, I suppose, never completely healed, although it disappeared to all intents and purposes when I was in my sophomore year, when my feelings of inferiority and jealousy were relieved by my friendship with Roger and Tom, who, being seniors, made me feel more important. I early loved to especially read exciting tales of valiant knights and fair ladies and dreamed beautiful, fantastic dreams of myself as a great hero. Since then I have lived in a semi-dream world of shadows. Even now I daydream excessively in more or less the same vein, willingly forsaking the humdrum of reality for the beauty and familiar comfort of my dreams. Great music and my writing are escape valves, although these I consider primarily as instruments of my personal salvation, and my almost passionate love of music is very profoundly connected with my religion. For example, Beethoven's Fifth Symphony is to me far more than a collection of pleasing sounds; it is the flawless expression of God's Love of triumphant hope and faith and goodness, and a magnificent picture of the human soul rising above despair and sin, hate and fear, to meet God on His holy mountains, on the very heights of spiritual ecstasy. Great music, then, has particularly influenced my life and thought, although I heartily detest much modern music, especially "rock 'n' roll" and the trash that Elvis Presley sings. Too, although I am not by any stretch of the imagination a good Christian, my religion has exerted a powerful and, I hope, growing influence on me. I have gained a tremendous amount of meaning for my life at religious youth camps. Of all the things that have enriched and enhanced my life, I think that my religion has come to mean the most to me.

Two people who have particularly influenced me have been the Rev. Mr. J. Edison Pike and Francis, who first interested me in the Episcopal Church and who helped me immeasurably in developing my faith. The person that has inspired me the most, and whom I have loved more than most other friends, was a very wonderful and courageous little lady who died of cancer this last summer. . . .

Autobiography II, 1963

1. The man who has most influenced me was my father, whose sacrificial practice of medicine and deep concern for human pain, whether organic or psychic, early shaped my conviction that self-fulfillment lies in service. I learned from him that a day's work never ends and that, because of the ubiquity of need and suffering, possessions are an embarrassment. The head of my department in college taught me craftsmanship in study and criticism, and he communicated to me something of his passion for the beautiful. The director of my college glee club, a mystic of sorts, revealed to me the life and consequences of faith. It was he who first led me to take seriously the total and startling experience of the new man in Christ.

I spent the summer following my freshman year in high school at the New England Music Camp. This experience opened to me a world of beauty, discipline, and purposeful community which has seemed a sort of Eden ever since. My father's death during my junior year in college precipitated an attack of anxiety which demanded intensive self-scrutiny and a thorough reconstruction of my life. I was thereby prepared for a renewal of faith last year and a recognition of vocation. My younger sister's year-long hospitalization for emotional illness has provided a testing ground for unconditional love and my own renewal.

My seminal literary influences were the Arthurian legends, novels typified by *The Cardinal*, the plays of Maxwell Anderson and O'Neill, and the Gospels. In his *Portrait of the Artist as a Young Man*, James Joyce first exposed me to the magic of language, concept, and knowledge. In the works of Dostoevski, Kafka, Sartre, and Camus, I have explored the meaninglessness prevalent in modern life and the limitations of humanism. Dostoevski, particularly, prepared the way for later religious development. John Hospers' *Introduction to Philosophical Analysis* impressed on me the convenience of analytic thought and the need for precision in discourse. Morison's *Who Moved the Stone?* encouraged me last year to reexamine my dissent. In the works of C. S. Lewis, both critical and apologetic, I found confirmation of the cogency as well as the necessity of faith. Recently, Dom Gregory Dix, in his *Shape of the Liturgy*, has invigorated my conviction of the centrality of the Holy Eucharist in Christian experience. The Gospel of Saint John has changed my life and thought more than any other writing I know.

2. My most interesting experiences in college were academic, particularly my studies in American literature, the classics, Shakespeare, analytic chemistry and biology, the fine arts, the English Romantics, and the literature of the Absurd. I had several cherished friends with whom I could share ideas, discoveries in the arts, intellectual and spiritual birth pangs, and increasing hostility to the military system. They were crucial to my happiness, and they stimulated my first conscious notions of mature friendship. I was involved in a number of extracurricular activities, the most important of which seemed to me to be the glee club and the college newspaper. As editorial editor of the latter, I was especially concerned with increasing military interference in study habits and in (what seemed to me) essentially collegiate areas of cadet life.

3. My strengths are intelligence and sensitivity, conscientiousness, honesty, introspection, critical perception, communicability, sympathy, and empathy. I am quick to see a need and anxious to help. Although I am a fairly keen student of motives, I should rather assure than judge. I have some skill in assisting people to understand themselves. Perhaps because of an intense awareness of my own limitations, I am decidedly more inclined to generosity than to aggression. I am almost invariably courteous, and I take very seriously the invitation to go a second mile.

My weaknesses are insecurity and a consequent lack of initiative, excessive concern with external opinion, frequent and almost paralyzing doubt, an inhibiting consciousness of appearances, perfectionism, and procrastination. I have had a dangerous tendency to overextend myself, with disastrous results to conflicting commitments and to myself.

I should say that the poise between my strengths and my weaknesses is delicate. I am constrained to suspect that many of my strengths are actuated by vanity, by a need to be loved and approved,* by a fear of aggression and anger—in short, by anxiety. I am beginning, however, to grasp the significance of the fact that anxiety is a reversible equation of self-worship and self-loathing. I am thereby reminded of the need for Grace, and I am learning to place my trust solely in It for the redemption of my own paradoxical nature. I am convinced that this is the only "strength" in which I may dare to rely.

4. I am most deeply concerned about the anxiety which seems, more than in any other era, to be the plague of our own. Though the blindness and the sin of other times stand in sharper relief, our own seem to me to be more deadly because more subtle. In our emancipation from traditional values, I wonder if we are not destroying ourselves. I am horrified by the evidence of increasing mental illness. Where psychiatry, of course, must bear much of the curative burden, I believe the Church must address Herself to many of the causes. I am bitterly opposed to racial prejudice, with which I have had some experience. Though I recognize the need for profit-seeking enterprise, I cannot happily tolerate the proximity of conspicuous waste and undernourished children (I should extend "proximity" to the ends of the earth). I am repelled by the valuation of material acquisition in our life. In our pursuit of gadgets and toys, we are profligate. The quest for status, like the desire to forget, is a frightening symptom of our spiritual orphanage. Our national vices are becoming tyrannous, not the least of which are narcotism, alcoholism, and marital subversion. There seems to me to be only a degree of sophistication in the distinction between victimizing a man by force and so crippling his spirit that he must repudiate both his responsibility and his freedom. Although I cannot deny the virtues of defense, I am appalled at the proportion of the gross international product devoted to military capability. When it is unleashed, it scars all mankind; when it is not, it usurps the

---

* I have attempted to observe this in my Sunday-school class. Perhaps I exaggerate the relationship between seeking to be loved and being loved. But my love is far from disinterested.

rightful use and sharing of our talents and our resources. I believe capital punishment to be depraved and our penal system in grave need of reform if it is to be effective.

5. It is the mission of the visible Church to restore men to the relationship with God exemplified and made possible by Christ. I believe quite literally that the Church, visible and invisible, militant and triumphant, is the living Body of Christ. As such, I understand Her to be partly human and material, partly divine and mystical. In the continual offering of each to the other, through sacrament and witness, I conceive of the Church as the locus of the Kingdom on earth. For this reason I think we are responsible to the whole man, political and economic as well as meditative. I recognize the Church as the custodian and interpreter of Holy Scripture and of sacred tradition, and I believe Her to be the ultimate community of faith and restoration. I must lament Her fragmentation and plead for Her unity. I believe the clergy to be called out of the laity to minister to it through the sacraments, prayer, teaching, counseling, and example. I conceive the priest's first responsibility to be to Christ, then to the faithful, and finally to society.

6. My objectives in entering theological studies are several. First, I should like to prepare myself for Holy Orders and for an intelligent, spiritually disciplined exercise of my ministry. But I am painfully conscious that I must work out the salvation of my own soul. As a layman I find it difficult to live my faith when it is choked with doubt—and thrice difficult to preach it. My belief is not always strong, my knowledge is uneven, and I am curious. My peripheral explorations of theology have been incalculably rewarding as well as pleasant. I should like now to explore more fully. I am eager to nourish my own spiritual life in a community of students and teachers dedicated to the same ends. Finally, I should like to lay the groundwork for possible graduate study in one of the theological disciplines.

J. DANIELS

Jonathan Daniels:
Letters

The following are excerpts from letters written by Jon Daniels to members of his family and to friends during the last three years of his life, commencing October 3, 1962.

To Carlton Russell:
     . . . Gradually, surely, mysteriously, wonderfully, my faith is growing. The intellect . . . must often be satisfied before it can be made to help rather than hinder, and yet it takes so much more (and, of course, so much "less") than this. But I think I am growing, even when sometimes obedience seems to suffer as faith stretches its wings. . . .

     I am increasingly distressed (thanks to a fresh batch of evidence) at the differences between *agapé* and *eros*. Disinterested love is so cussed reluctant, and passionate love so (equally cussed) headstrong. One must constantly be commanded into being, and the other whipped into discretion. Still worse, it seems to me, *agapé* is at present, I am afraid, least to be prized when it becomes spontaneous, for the very reason that it seems a triumph and, in the moment of gratitude, passes without notice into recklessness. And, on the other hand, when *eros* loses its spontaneity it becomes dead. We love either too little or too much. As C. S. Lewis so rightly observes, "We must get over wanting to be needed." And what, in a way, is needing another person but wanting to be needed? What is jealousy but this? What is this but *eros*? I catch myself, for example, trying to trap ———— into needing me—and resent anybody else who, in turn, needs her. Must we not in the love of Christ (what I must insist with myself is the only real love) work always and solely for the perfect freedom of the beloved? Then what am I doing when I "love" ————? Staring, I fear, into the opacity of my own semen. Narcissus is a short-sighted bastard. How long, how long O Lord, must Israel remain in bondage? I ask that Christ will beat this heart and mind into submission, and even in the moment of prayer the hands that pray caress the filth of the tyrant. The right hand shall not know the left? As I attempt with one to negotiate the final surrender of my will, the other pats into place its new defenses. Without Grace, the cause would indeed be lost. I am more cunning than I knew. Pray for me, as I do for you. . . .

KEENE, NEW HAMPSHIRE
OCTOBER 3, 1962

To James Wilson:
. . . I am planning pretty definitely to be a priest—God willing. Whether I'll then go get a doctorate and teach or tackle, for example, a slum parish I simply don't know at this point. I am excited about the theological enterprise, reading some great people, and having an uncomfortable, glorious glimpse now and then of what the Cross of Jesus Christ calls us to. I think I am gradually becoming more committed to His strange work and Person. But I have so, so much to learn about the obedient service in which is our only perfect freedom. And miles to go—and reams to read—before I sleep!

EPISCOPAL THEOLOGICAL SCHOOL
APRIL, 1964

To his sister Emily:
. . . This whole year is the most important of my life to date—simply in terms of me as a person in the process of becoming. Field work has recently become something I do not understand —but anyway, I am beginning to think very seriously (almost constantly) about the parish ministry—perhaps necessarily, especially the inner-city church and its ramifications. Spent Sunday afternoon at a reform school near Providence, which drove another nail. I have so much to learn—a bitter, bitter failure with one of my prospective J. D.'s Sunday morning—female, absolutely hostile, alienated from everything and everybody. We are

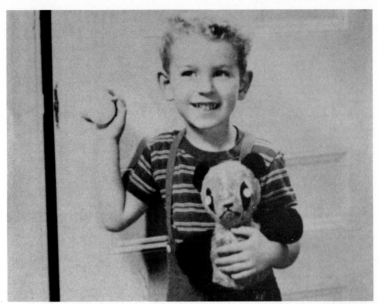

Jon spent his preschool years in the South, and was later to write how the vivid childhood memories of this time led him to consider that region his "adopted home."

The Daniels family, Christmas 1954: Dr. Philip Daniels, beloved and respected town physician; Constance Daniels, a high school French teacher; younger sister Emily, and Jonathan.

As a VMI cadet Jonathan seemed to thrive on the austerity and discipline of student life.

Disguised as a beatnik in "The Bomb" (VMI yearbook), 1961.

Jon escorted Abby MacDonald to his ring ceremony at VMI in the fall of 1959.

JONATHAN MYRICK DANIELS
"Jon"

KEENE, NEW HAMPSHIRE

English, Air Force—Private 4, 3, 2, 1; *Distinguished Academic Student* 3, 2, 1; *Who's Who Among Students in American Colleges and Universities;* Officers of the Guard Association; Yankee Club 4; Fencing 4; Canterbury Club 4, 3; Episcopal Cadet Vestry 3; *The Cadet* 3, 2, Exchange Editor 2, Editorial Editor 1; Glee Club 4, 3, 2; Timmins Music Society 2, 1, Director 2; R. E. Dixon English Society 3, 2, Program Chairman 2, President 1.

The presence of a New Hampshire Yankee in a southern military college has for four years roused the curiosity of his Dixie colleagues. His idiosyncrasies, carefully nourished in a dank northern clime, have been assiduously scrutinized. Eventually, admiration was coupled with curiosity. Jon's verbal ability and facile command of the English tongue are renowned. Jon's insatiable thirst for nectar of bean is rivalled only by his thirst for knowledge. The wide range of his courses explodes the myth that an English major cannot dabble successfully in science, attested by his distinction in sideline investigations of biology and chemistry, as well as history. An occasional bout at the local mead halls restores the vigor required for the daily frenzy. His purposeful egoism is balanced by unfailing tact and generosity. For these qualities we admire him.

VMI yearbook profile highlights his devotion to "nectar of bean" (coffee) and his success in a variety of academic and social pursuits.

At the EDS lectern, summer 1965.

A photo of a Dallas County family, taken by Jon in July, 1965.

Sharing a chuckle with Shey-anne Webb, one of the children of Selma whom Jon tutored.

Jon with Judith Upham and their young charges at St. Paul's Episcopal Church in Selma.

A relaxed though pensive Jonathan, one month before his death.

No.	Nat'l.	W	Comp.		
Henry W. Vickery	Sex M	C.E.	Leaving Scene	7.C.TA	
	Age 47	C.H.	of accident		
	Height	Wt.			
No.	Nat'l. W	Comp.	Held for		
Jonathan Vaniels	Sex M	C.E.	City of		
	Age 26	C.H.	Fort Deposit		
alias Daniels	Height	Wt.			
No.	Nat'l. B	Comp.	Held for		
Willie Vaughn	Sex M	C.E.	City of		
	Age 21	C.H.	Fort Deposit		
	Height	Wt.			
No.	Nat'l. W	Comp.	Assault		
Robert James Vinger	Sex M	C.E.	with intent	E. Holm	
	Age 24	C.H.	to Murder		
	Height 5''	Wt.			
No.	Nat'l. W	Comp.	Attempt & Arla		
Bobie Vandiver	Sex F	C.E.	to		
	Age 55	C.H.	Distill		
	Height	Wt.			

Police ledger recording Jon's arrest, with the curious "Vaniels (alias Daniels)" notation.

The Cash Store, Hayneville, Alabama, site of the shooting.

Ruby Sales (center), the teenager Jon pushed to the ground and out of gunfire. She is now a community activist in Washington, D.C.

Jonathan's inscription on the Civil Rights Memorial, Montgomery, Alabama.

Photographs Courtesy Of:
Larry Benaquist and Bill Sullivan
Directors, The Jonathan Daniels Film Project

The Birmingham News, Birmingham, Alabama

fighting a strange battle, which somehow love must win. . . .
But, maybe because the failure was so terrible, I came away knowing something I had never known before about love and faith. We
who call ourselves Christians must learn a little better the way
of the Cross. Somehow, that is where God and life and love *are*
—and where triumphant. It is so hard to learn—but that is what
our Lord has called us to. . . .
EPISCOPAL THEOLOGICAL SCHOOL
MAY, 1964

To his Mother:
. . . I am fine. Questions rise in a gale, and I am glad! I am
taking another long look at myself, and society and so on. I am a
(somewhat radical) Christian, loosely (very loosely) devoted to
the institutional Church, very much wrapped up in theological,
religious, or ultimate questions, conscious of my own needs and
talents. I am increasingly suspicious of the ordained ministry
(and of the psychopathology often behind it)—and increasingly
open to psychiatry. So far so good. . . .
WILLARD STATE HOSPITAL
WILLARD, NEW YORK
JULY 7, 1964

To his Mother:
. . . Yes—I am thinking very seriously about hitting every loan
fund in a 1,000 square miles and going into *medicine*—specifically
psychiatry. The Bug has never left my system, and everything I
know about me and believe about Reality makes me think more
surely that my ministry is *there*. Practically: am considering medical school for year after this. Plan to drop Greek and preaching
for something more supportive to 2/3'ds of a theologically educated layman! Would love to be priested first, but don't think
there's time. . . .
WILLARD STATE HOSPITAL
WILLARD, NEW YORK
JULY 23, 1964

To John Gallagher:

. . . I am increasingly aware that my three years at ETS are primarily a chapter in my salvation-history. In my priority of values and vocational goals, I am called into this community first to become a mature Christian person, then a Christian priest, and then (hopefully) a Christian scholar. I am aware that I have a ministry here to some of my fellows and their wives, and I am thankful that some have recognized their ministry to me. There are glorious moments when in groups of two or three we love as we have been loved, and when they happen, the times are redeemed. But the groups of two or three erect their own walls and wither as they must. As a larger community, we are open enough with our sins of petty hostility and academic pretense. But we are less willing to communicate our faith and the new life we have found and continue to find in the Cross. I think sometimes we are afraid to admit that our religion is anything other than a (rather precarious) intellectual venture. I think I know why—but I can testify with assurance that the causes are not invincible. If we dare not suspend our critical activities *here* to confess and explore the lonely, glorious absurdity of our life in Christ, we shall have a difficult time being faithful shepherds. Our cynicism is revealing. . . .

EPISCOPAL THEOLOGICAL SCHOOL
FALL, 1964

To Carlton and Lorna Russell:

. . . I am tickled to death with and for you both. And proleptically thankful for the quiet miracle you have already begun to share with a new-old friend. You know you have my warmest and fondest good wishes. And, I suppose I don't need to say, my (God-given) envy! . . .

. . . the summer was instructive and challenging. I learned a great deal about listening and counseling, far more about myself. It was long and tedious much of the time, yet I loved some of my patients a great deal. The course in Brooklyn was in crime and delinquency, given by the probation department of the supreme court of New York. Some of the material was a little old hat, but I found most helpful—and fascinating—the sessions on the addictions. Among other things, we spent an evening at the narcotics halfway house out on the end of Staten Island ("Daytop Lodge," I believe). . . .

. . . I am excited about my work, though really a little overworked. Between overloading and my increasingly complicated preparations for taking over as manager of the bookstore here (a stimulating but awful job), I am quietly frantic. The courses are great, aside from Greek and homiletics. Theology (at long last I'm getting around to reading Tillich *et al.*), Synoptics, Pentateuch, and a course in church history at Harvard Divinity School ('Kingdom of God: Church-State Theory in the Ancient and Medieval Church') are all splendid.

I am doing field work in Providence again—on Saturdays alone this year. Kind of exciting: a tenuously pastoral relationship (I trust they don't know it) with a team of kids from Brown, Pembroke, and the Rhode Island School of Design, who are running a rather complex program for the children in the neighborhood of the mission where I worked last year. I hope that once my supervisor and his family move into a house in the area, which the Diocese has bought, I shall be able to work Saturday nights with the teenagers who are a tempestuous lot. . . .

Carlton—the family of man. Yes. I think I can guess at the beauty and the holiness of what you mean. I know you will build well, the two of you. Your wonderful gifts are both God's blessing and His imperative.

I am glad you are coming into this Church, old friend. For all her sins (and they are many), exciting and blessed things are happening in her midst. She has been given much in the way of intelligence and creative resources (you are such a gift), and her task is therefore enormous. Sacrament and Word still speak to us and through us, though sometimes it seems as if we are consecrated to blocking the channels. You will be welcome—and needed for the common task. I'm thrilled that you're coming! . . .

EPISCOPAL THEOLOGICAL SCHOOL

EARLY OCTOBER, 1964

To his Mother:

. . . The march was *enormous* and went off quite successfully. King gave a moving address—he is certainly one of the greatest men of our times. Judy and I saw Professor Guthrie there, also Bill Schneider and three fellows from ETS. There were any number of people from the Boston area—a professor I had at Harvard, the Harvard University preacher (Dr. Price, a member of the faculty at the Virginia Seminary who also helps to teach liturgics this semester, one of my courses) among many, many others. Judy and I got back after the march had started (we met it just outside of Selma), so we spent a day or two fixing our library, getting some rest, etc. Tuesday night I stood security guard at the encampment. Wednesday night my cohorts and I rejoined the march at the camp just outside Montgomery. A little to my disappointment—which reflects some inadequacies in my acceptance of humanity, I guess—the evening was devoted to entertainment by a host of celebrities who had come in support of the demonstration. They were good, some of them kind of thrilling. But I began to feel a little as if I were at a circus. That feeling has been compounded by the officiousness of many of the white students who have recently arrived (and hopefully now departed). The latter belong mostly to SNCC (Student Nonviolent Coordinating Committee), and they are a very different bunch from the Negro leadership of SCLC. The problem is not that they're white; it's that they're immature (as, of course, they can't help being), just a little arrogant from past success, and obviously not indigenous. I suppose I can't expect everybody to be of the caliber of Dr. King and his staff—but anything less than real leadership in this movement can only do harm, both within and without the ranks. On the other hand, I am so grateful for the men and women in this beloved community who, despite educational and cultural starvation, are able to think clearly and honestly. And who are brave enough not only to risk life and limb in the moment of flamboyant action, but to give up their jobs and incomes. The white community is apparently beginning to feel the effects of the boycott as well as the demonstrations.

Judy and I spent Saturday night (or early Sunday morning) at the Canterbury House at (Negro) Atlanta University. We went to Communion there and stayed for breakfast afterwards. Father Scott and the students we met were wonderfully good to us and very delightful people. . . .

Tomorrow one of our priest friends will celebrate Holy Communion for us. . . . Then, in little groups, we and the kids who have been reading Morning and Evening Prayer with us every day will make another quiet attempt to integrate St. Paul's Church. There is at least a remote chance that they'll let us in this time. Hope so—that could be a very important first step. Judy and I had planned to go every Sunday—just the two of us—in hopes that eventually somebody would make some sort of gesture in our direction. But Father Samuel is probably right that we ought to take the kids, especially since they really would like to go. . . .

SELMA, ALABAMA
MARCH 26, 1965

To Mary Elizabeth Macnaughtan:

. . . In a strange way, this beloved community within the Negro compound have become my people—much as, in a very special way, you, dear Mary, are my people. I drove every mile away from you with anguished longing for you. Yet something had happened to me in Selma which meant I had to come back. I could not stand by in benevolent dispassion any longer without compromising everything I know and love and value. The imperative was too clear, the stakes were too high, my own identity was called too nakedly into question. I realize that the vision came to me as an individual person—it is not something which can be spelled out in a policy for everybody I know. But I had been blinded by what I saw here (and everywhere), and the road to Damascus led, for me, back here. A very dear friend of mine in Cambridge, the chaplain to Episcopalians at Harvard and Radcliffe, said, "You must go, Jon, wherever you find your Jerusalem. Yours and mine may not be the same. But wherever yours is, there you must go." Another friend, the beloved New Testament professor I've told you about, who at first was against our coming back, told one of his classes the day before we left: "When the call comes, you have to drop what you're doing and go. Sometimes the call comes at the least convenient moment you can imagine. But whenever it comes, you must go." Through all the bitter moments of doubt since I left (and they have been many) those words shine with untarnished brilliance. Though I have many misgivings, though at the moment I can't imagine that I have anything to give of any significance, I know with heart, mind, and soul that the Holy Spirit has picked me up by the scruff of the neck. When that happened, my life could not remain the same. Though I cannot guess precisely where I am being driven, I have the haunting feeling again and again that I am flying with the mightiest Wind in the world at my back. I hope you understand what I'm trying to say. I'm not entirely sure that I understand myself. . . .

SELMA, ALABAMA
MARCH 29, 1965

To Mary Elizabeth Macnaughtan:

. . . We are slowly getting into motion here. Communication amongst us is improving, and some sort of organization is emerging. Of course Dr. King's outfit is still calling the shots—but Atlanta's a long way off. He, by the way, is one of the greatest men I've ever laid eyes on. I pray he doesn't get bumped off—the whole country needs him. The snipers are still doing their dirty work—a hacked up black body was found today in a nearby county. One of my good friends here, an Episcopal priest from L.A.—and an activist if ever I saw one—got two threats on his life today from members of the sheriff's posse. I wonder how long the southern white will get away with rule by terror. Sometimes I think this place isn't even civilized. Sure is strange country—sort of like being deep within enemy lines.

Plans for the future here (in our somewhat independent organization, which is nevertheless led by a member of the SCLC Staff) include steps toward improving hygiene (exterminating the army of cockroaches!) in the Negro federal project, a birth control project, continuing negotiation with members of the white power structure (Judy and I have made a start, even if we don't think much has happened), the nurture of an indigenous protest movement at all-Negro Selma University. . . .

I've—obviously—gotten sidetracked. We got involved in the Camden ruckus (managed to get myself amply tear-gassed leading a march there last Wednesday), which kept us busy through last Friday. The civil authorities were *very* anxious, however, to avoid what began increasingly to look like the beginnings of another Selma, so Friday they were most cooperative toward our protest march on city hall.

Sunday we had one heck of a time getting into early Communion at St. Paul's with our black kiddoes. They seem to be getting used to our presence at Morning Prayer, but evidently the thought of contaminating their holy cup is just too much for them. Anyway, they called the cops on us and refused to let us into the church—until the rector summoned the guts to announce that even if it meant his job, they had to admit us. We were made to sit in the back, and we had to wait until last. But we went to Palm Sunday Communion, by golly! When we went back later for Morning Prayer with the batch of kids who hadn't wanted to go to Holy Communion, a man going into church with us greeted us with "You god-damned scum. . . ." The rector looked as if somebody had been cussing him out ever since we'd left the early service, but he was friendly afterwards and actually asked me to wait and talk with him. Judy and I (who are now the contacts for John Morris of ESCRU in Atlanta) have agreed not to ruin their Easter by bringing the kids next Sunday. I feel bad about running the risk of disappointing the kids, but agree with my superiors that this concession may be an important guarantee of our good will. So Judy and I will go alone to an early service—I'm preaching at our family's Negro Methodist Church later in the morning.

This afternoon Judy and I had a most fruitful talk with a man and his wife (who are communicants at St. Paul's). They actually invited us into their home and fed us Cokes and cookies! They were very gracious, if not quite so liberal as they think. They don't go for my hero Dr. King at all, deplore the boycott, and are generally suspicious of the movement. But we each tried, I think, to listen to one another with something like compassionate understanding. I suspect that love will have to be crucified many times before the battle is over, so I may as well get used to the frustration. There are still moments when I'd like to get a high-powered rifle and take to the woods, but more and more strongly I am beginning to feel that ultimately the revolution to which I am committed is the way of the Cross. Something in me doesn't like insisting that my black brothers walk it any longer, yet I must remain faithful to the One Who above all others is my Leader. And I am convinced that in the long run the "strategy of love" is the only one that will bring real health and reconciliation into this mess. I'm glad that Dr. King walks the same road (which he does, however forceful he sometimes must be). Yet I sure understand when Negroes get impatient with "nonviolence." "How long, O Lord, how Long?"

You should see me in my seminarian's collar and dungaree suit!—I look like a jailbird from way back. With my dark suit, however, I must say I look most proper. Will have to send you some pictures when I get them developed. There ought to be some wonderful ones of our kids. I bought a super-duper camera, by the way, cartridge-loading, automatic film advance (a tiny spring motor), electric eye, and a distance rangefinder. It cost a small fortune, but it's very fast and very accurate. We got it primarily to record violence if and when it occurs (when we're not the recipients, that is). But it's going to be fun to have good pictures of our friends and various bits of local color. . . .

SELMA, ALABAMA
APRIL 12, 1965

To *Molly D. Thoron:*
    . . . I think I have grown in the last month (though scarcely around the waistline!—I'm starved most of the time, as I suspect are the dear people with whom I live, and I suppose losing a pound here and there). Emotionally, intellectually, spiritually I have had to respond to many and varied stimuli. At first, I think I should gladly have procured a high-powered rifle and taken to the woods

—to fight the battle as the Klansmen do. I was very, very angry: with white people (fascinating how, under conditions like these, one can almost totally identify with another race as being in a significant way one's own people), with the system by which the middle-class power structure (even very fine people) willfully blind themselves to human need and whatever else they'd rather not see, with the faithlessness of the churches, with the sickness of our civilization. My hostility lasted really until last week. I think it was when I got tear-gassed leading a march in Camden that I began to change. I saw that the men who came at me were themselves not free: it was not that cruelty was so sweet to them (though I'm afraid sometimes it is), *but that they didn't know what else to do.* Even though they were white and hateful and my enemy, they were human beings, too. I found myself feeling a kind of grim affection for them, at least a love that was real and "existential" rather than abstract. Four weeks ago I had realized that as a Christian, as a "soldier of the Cross," I was totally free —at least free to give my life, if that had to be, with joy and thankfulness and eagerness for the Kingdom no longer hidden from my blind eyes. With the glory of the Cross in my blood and my black brothers at my side, there was no longer anything to fear in all of Creation except my own blindness. Last week in Camden I began to discover a new freedom in the Cross: freedom to love the enemy. And in that freedom, the freedom (without hypocrisy) to will and to try to set him free. I am so thankful that now as I go about my primary business of attempting to negotiate with the white power structure in the local Episcopal church (which we have integrated, at least in token form), there is a new factor —I rather think a new Presence—in our conversations: the "strategy of love." . . . Certainly compassion, the attempt to understand, genuine concern for the "enemy" will accomplish more for real integration of the races than belligerence. . . .

SELMA, ALABAMA
APRIL 15, 1965

The following two letters were written to the Rt. Rev. C. J. Carpenter by Jon Daniels and Judy Upham protesting the treatment which they and their friends received at St. Paul's Church, Selma, Alabama:

April 21, 1965

Right Reverend and Dear Sir:

Shortly after your visit on April 15 with the rector and vestry of St. Paul's Church, Selma, we were advised by the rector, the Rev. T. Franklin Mathews, that you had directed that our racially mixed group of worshippers could not be excluded from the Eucharist, but that the ushers might seat us at their own discretion. Mr. Mathews indicated that this policy would subsequently be followed.

At the early service of Holy Communion on Easter Sunday we were seated in the left rear pew, six pews behind the nearest communicants in front of us, and without access to the central aisle. Not only were we thus the last to be communicated, but we were furthermore forced to remain in our seats until after the rest of the congregation had communicated and returned to their seats. Only when the altar rail and the several aisles were empty were we finally allowed to approach the altar.

As we had approached the church before the service we were met by an usher, who insisted that we not bring any Negroes to the festal celebration at eleven. When we left the church at the conclusion of the service, though we were among the first to approach the rector, we were nearly the last to whom he gave his attention. We made several quiet attempts to gain his attention, and each time he rather studiously ignored us until at last he could presumably do so no longer. Thus we were forced to wait five minutes or more to wish him a good morning and a blessed Easter.

We and the Negro children worshipping with us have repeatedly been the objects of obscene remarks and insults by some of the congregation as we have entered and left the church and the recipients of hostile glares by others, though a small minority have been extremely gracious. Though Mr. Mathews has been most cordial during most of our conversations with him, he requested on Holy Saturday that, as our ecumenical interest ought to indicate that the Episcopal Church was not a necessity for us, we cease worshipping at St. Paul's and worship instead at a local Negro church of another denomination.

Though the policy attributed to you and the attitude displayed by the parish may indeed approximate the letter of the canon, they scarcely fulfill its spirit. We are distressed at what appears to be a deliberate breach of the conditions cited in the Invitation to Holy Communion—and a compromise of the gospel, as well.,

Surely the gospel, as it is delivered to this Church and proclaimed at her altars and pulpits, calls for a charity, a witness, and a living reconciliation that the racial policy of St. Paul's Church currently negates. As Episcopalians, as representatives of ESCRU, as seminarians, as members of the Holy Catholic Church we must lament the policy you are represented as having enunciated and urge you to use your considerable influence to correct the situation. This we cordially and respectfully ask you to do.

With every good wish for you and the prayer that the Risen Lord will bless you now and always as you go about the difficult task of reconciling the children of God to the purposes of God, we have the honor to remain

Yours obediently in Him,
Jonathan Myrick Daniels
E.T.S., Class of 1966, New Hampshire

Judith Elizabeth Upham
E.T.S., Class of 1967, Missouri

April 28, 1965

Right Reverend and Dear Sir:

Thank you for your letter of the twenty-third, in response to ours of the twenty-first.

Though we talked with you yesterday at Carpenter House and were therefore able to refer to the concerns of our previous letter, we note with regret that you felt it necessary to deal only with the issue of obscene remarks made to us by communicants of St. Paul's in Selma. As you must be aware from our previous letter and from your conversation with Father Stines and us yesterday, there are considerably more distressing issues at St. Paul's, of which obscenity is only an obvious symptom. The same is true, of course, of Mr. Mathews' subtle discourtesy after the early service of Holy Communion on Easter Sunday. That is scarcely the reason why we drove to Birmingham to see you.

Because we related to you *verbatim* yesterday two of the many obscene remarks to which we alluded in passing in our previous letter and which you ask us to cite in yours, we ask to spare you their reproduction on paper. Should there be any need for documentation in the future, we shall of course comply with your further request. It goes without saying that we accept your gracious apology and that we appreciate your concern.

We fail, however, to see how you can investigate the instances of obscenity to which we have alluded or deal very effectively with the possibility of their recurrence in the future. Furthermore, as we have said above, obscenity is only a symptom of the complicated sickness that afflicts the life and the witness of St. Paul's.

It is clear to us, as it is to others in the Church, that you could deal with the more critical issues we have mentioned and even with the sickness itself. Both the authority and the responsibility to do so accrue to you in your capacity as Diocesan. Your unwillingness to do so will occasion grave concern and sorrow throughout the Church, as it does for us.

Contrary to your repeated assertions yesterday, the issue has little to do with the subjectivity of hurt feelings—whether *ours*, as you insist, or those of white Episcopalians in the black belt. The issue is the objective fact of the policy of racial discrimination practiced by St. Paul's, Selma, and endorsed yesterday by the Diocesan of Alabama. Please remember, sir, that the seating policy of St. Paul's, *as it applies specifically to us*, has been explicitly announced to us by the rector of that parish as being discriminatory in purpose.

Insistence that Negroes be the last to receive the Chalice at the Sacrament is an overt violation of the "equal rights and status" clause of Canon 16, Section 4. Therefore we cannot accede to your insistence that we "go to church with eyes closed and just worship the Lord without looking for faults." The terms of the canon and the teaching of the Church force us to regard as irrelevant in the present case your insistence that we wait humbly and thankfully for our turn at the Holy Table. The issue is not a question of our humility or even of our obedience; if it were, our response, of course, would be very different. The issue is simply and starkly that the measures you employ to facilitate the "humility" of our black brothers constitute a clear-cut instance of racial discrimination. This we must resist, out of obedience to the gospel itself, with every means and resource that the gospel offers us. Genuine humility implies for us, as white Christians, steadfast refusal to accept any violation of either the letter or the spirit of this canon. There is a difference between humility and humiliation.

We respectfully protest the discriminatory policy practiced at St. Paul's and lament your refusal yesterday to take any action. It is our earnest hope that you will reconsider your position. Perhaps that will be, for the Diocese of Alabama, another step on the way of the Cross.

Contrary to your insistence that the tone of our previous letter was petty and resentful, we write you, now as then, with deep respect and with every good wish. Like Mr. Mathews and our parish family in Selma, you remain in our prayers.

Thank you for good coffee yesterday! Please give our regards to your secretary and to Mr. Yon, whom we enjoyed meeting.

Yours respectfully in Christ,
Jonathan Myrick Daniels
Judith Elizabeth Upham

To his Mother:

So good to talk with you the other night. Have been busy since then! Perhaps I had been (with Judy and Father Stines from ESCRU in Atlanta) to see Bishop Carpenter in Birmingham when I called you? Judy and I sent off a second letter to him, charging him (respectfully) with a violation of Canon 16, Sec. 4. Then Father Morris called, and (to make a long story short) he, Father Stines, and another ESCRU priest flew to Birmingham yesterday morning. Judy and I met them (about eight-thirty), and after a pleasant breakfast the five of us proceeded to the Diocesan headquarters downtown, where we picketed for a little over four hours. Signs read SLAVE GALLERY REVIVED, BISHOP SANCTIONS SEGREGATED SLAVERY IN SELMA CHURCH, CHURCH CAMPS STILL SEGREGATED. The two that Judy and I carried had a big crucifix, half black and half white, with a Negro and a Caucasian on either side of a barbed wire fence intersecting with the Cross at a diagonal, and the words SEGREGATION . . . SEPARATION.

The decision re this summer still hasn't been made. I'm not sure what He wants—but I sure have learned that my life is no longer my own. The immediate decision of course hooks up with a much bigger one (that I hate to admit I ought to be deciding). Am I going to pursue an academic ministry or am I called to be a slum-priest-type? Abstractly I can still shore up the defenses for academia. But viscerally the argument runs the other way. I'd so like to be a pastor—and actively involved in the social revolution(s). Also the old qt. of the Catholic Church rears its ugly/lovely head again. But I guess that's another story. Anyway—it can wait! More soon. . . .

SELMA, ALABAMA
MAY 1, 1965

To the Rev. William J. Schneider:
. . . It goes without saying, I guess, that I'm interested in the kind of thing that St. Ann's Church is doing. Yet, at least on paper, I'm supposed to be committed to some sort of academic ministry after ordination. It may well be that I ought to do more intensive college work at this point—it is already clear to me that my vocational orientation has shifted decidedly from the groves of academe to the streets. I've got some stewing to do—and some praying. But I suppose the question won't be answered for some time. Yet I have a hunch. . . . I have a little more to learn of "radical obedience" (and of poverty and chastity, too, for that matter). It is so hard to give oneself up. And yet so essential. I think I used to want to be an academic to feed my pride (or perhaps only my vanity?). Whichever, I'm beginning to have second thoughts. The gospel is less and less a matter primarily of the intellect. And more and more a matter of living and dying and living anew. I don't know whether I will ever again have either the energy or the patience to play games. I haven't grown less sophisticated (I guess), but I have grown simpler—maybe because I'm tired and hungry most of the time. A day comes when the sinner

sees himself in the mirror, and the old pretenses and sophistries refuse to function any more. Conversion occurs again and again, and one is never quite the same even if the old man looks pretty well preserved. If it were not for Jerusalem, I think I should be nearly ready for the Trappists or some such. I'm not, and yet I know now as I've only half known before that I must learn to pray. Jerusalem. . . . I'm wondering again, with deep pain, if Rome lies en route—but that's another question. . . .

. . . I could spend most of my time just playing pastor here—there is so much to be done, and there are so few hands. The good ones, of course, are white and they don't care what happens to people here. I'd almost say to heck with keeping St. Paul's integrated if I could see a black priest here—educated and clinically trained—running his own mission. Oh well. I'll come home some day and bare my soul to you over a glass of Scotch. . . .

SELMA, ALABAMA
MAY, 1965

To Mary Elizabeth Macnaughtan:
. . . Technically, I haven't made my own decision—but the chances are about a thousand to one that I'll decide to come back. ESCRU wants me to come back, and I'm so well acclimated by now that it seems a shame to throw it all away. We would definitely be involved in the following: keeping St. Paul's integrated, talking informally with members of the white power structure whom I've encountered at or through St. Paul's (doctors, lawyers, judges, the rector, etc.), relating with kids and adults here in the Negro community (for instance, I have been working some with my family, specifically on their marital difficulties, the father's alcoholism, etc.), and just constituting the presence of the Church in the social revolution which is gathering strength here. Other potential activities might include tutoring both kids and adults in basic reading and writing skills, demonstrating (that's almost inevitable once in awhile: and you should have prepared in advance, *both physically and spiritually*, for the possibility of tear gas, arrest, and I suppose even for death, though that's a bit unlikely). It is true abstractly (as I see it) that no white outsider

here is entirely safe—and I feel very strongly that one should make a realistic estimate of what that means. I say this because I decided a long time ago that the Holy Spirit had brought me here, that I believe very firmly in the gospel and its faith, that my life is not my own but His—which means that before anything else I am a servant of Christ, however sinful I may also be —and that consequently the possibility of death, whether immediate or remote, cannot be a deciding factor for me. I can't decide all that for you—only you, on your own knees and out of the context of your own commitment to the Lord and His Kingdom, can make the "estimate" for yourself. You will find people here who are not Christians or even theists, who have dealt with the question of danger on other grounds. I have no other grounds, so can recommend only these. . . . You will surely find things, situations, decisions, and people here that you wouldn't like anywhere. That has been very true for me. You will also find wonderful work to be done and a situation in which (I assume from my own experience) you will grow in holiness and devotion to His service, in social consciousness, and in your own vision of what life will be for you. Offhand, I can't think of a more productive way for you or for any college student (or any Christian!) to spend a summer. . . . Also: rustling up people who haven't registered to vote yet. Perhaps also helping to administer food and clothing sent from the North. There are any number of programs that will be available (recreation, etc.) and you might want to work independently some of the time—for instance if you don't feel like picketing! . . .

SELMA, ALABAMA
MAY 1, 1965

To his Mother and his Grandmother Weaver:
 . . . Please don't worry about my stewings. I am not, though of course there is a certain amount of frustration. But there is indeed no rush about any of the questions—and my impetuous nature is unusually calm. Perhaps that's because I've had a good dose of some that aren't. . . . At any rate, the issues I raised are really fairly old ones, which have simply come into clearer focus here

(where pretense is folly, ambition a nuisance, and sin the curse that it really is). I am called first to be a saint, as we all are. The rest is incidental. . . .

SELMA, ALABAMA
MAY, 1965

This letter was written by Jon Daniels and Judy Upham to the Rev. John B. Morris, Executive Director, ESCRU:

In the interval since we last talked with you, we have had a long conversation with Mr. Mathews, the rector of St. Paul's in Selma, and Mr. Miller Childers, whom Mr. Mathews had asked to be present for our appointment. The conversation was frank, though for the most part very cordial, and mutually informative. Each side sought to explore the other's position, and there appeared to be some clarification of motives, concerns, and goals. Needless to say, there was little fundamental agreement on cultural and racial lines—or on methodology—yet there were indications on both sides of good faith and of serious commitment to Christian behavior.

Mr. Mathews took strenuous exception to the suggestion in the ESCRU statement of April 29, which we signed with the staff members with whom we picketed Diocesan headquarters in Birmingham, that St. Paul's is seeking to discard the common cup on a discriminatory basis. As you recall, our reference was to the commendation of intinction in the inserted instructions on the Holy Communion in the parish bulletin for the first Sunday after Easter. Mr. Mathews insisted that the insert had been composed some time ago, perhaps as much as six months ago, and appeared at this time only coincidentally. We agreed that perhaps he and St. Paul's had been misrepresented on this point and assured him that we would convey to you his dissatisfaction.

Mr. Mathews also insisted that his discourtesy to us on Easter Sunday after the early service of Holy Communion was not intentional. He objected to our passing mention of the incident in one of our letters to Bishop Carpenter, feeling that we should first have discussed the matter with him. Though frankly astonished that what appeared to us to have been so studied an avoidance could have been unintentional, we appreciated his feeling that we ought first to have expressed our reaction to him (as we have on other issues) and apologized. However, as we have discovered since our conversation with him that he has given to the Public Safety Director of Selma copies of our letters and statements to Bishop Carpenter, without notifying us, we are no longer precisely sure as to his feelings on the subject.

Since there were no ushers at the early service of Holy Communion this morning, the problem of enforced discriminatory seating did not arise. Half a dozen or more people were communicated after us, without apparent difficulty. After the service Mr. Mathews greeted the two of us and our Negro friend pleasantly.

We look forward to seeing you later this week. And to meeting your family! Our best to Father Stines and Father Dreisbach.

SELMA, ALABAMA

MAY 9, 1965

Memo to Carl Edwards:

We never got around to our discussion of freedom! I'm sorry. Perhaps the answer hinges on what one means by "freedom." There is the wide open, free-wheeling *abandon* of the gospel, the infectious *liberatedness* of a cause, the *abandonment* (?) of poverty, the *license* of irresponsibility, the *detachment* of the student, etc., etc., etc. Maybe all of these, in various combinations, are present in the "freedom" we are talking about. You know, I think, that I am inclined to be a little skeptical about *all* the "freedoms" which are not grounded in the "slavery" of His service. I'm a dogmatic cuss—but my own life experience nudges me in the direction of this skepticism.

See you some more. You will be in mind, heart, and prayers at ordination time. Congratulations and every good wish go with you. God bless. . . .

EPISCOPAL THEOLOGICAL SCHOOL

JUNE 22, 1965

This letter was written from prison on August 17. It was his last letter, and was received by his mother the day after he died.

August 17, 1965

Dearest Mum,

An eminently peculiar birthday card, but . . . I have been in jail ever since Sat.—the Lowndes County jail in Hayneville, after being transferred from Fort Deposit, where a bunch of us were arrested for picketing. (As a guntoting Cracker said to me when I observed that we had a constitutional right to picket, "You don't have any rights in Fort Deposit.") We are not being bailed out because we are seeking an injunction and trying to get our cases transferred to a federal court. The food is vile and we aren't allowed to bathe (whew!), but otherwise we are okay. Should be out in 2-3 days and back to work. As you can imagine, I'll have a tale or two to swap over our next martini! (This damned pencil is about an inch and a quarter long.) Getting some reading, thinking, discussing, speculating (and sleeping) done—though cussed little else.

The card I bought and the present will have to wait, I guess. But I sure will be thinking of you with love and prayers! Have a martini for me and a birthday that is gay in some fun way.

With much, much love,

Jon

p.s. Am horrified that I let August 6 go by. I *am* busy!

p.p.s. In addition to organizing, will be doing some (political) preaching at a revival when I get out! Ha!

Jonathan Daniels:
Papers

A Burning Bush   April, 1965

Reality is kaleidoscopic in the black belt. Now you see it; now you don't. The view is never the same. Climate is an affair of the soul as well as the body: today the sun sears the earth, and a man goes limp in its scorching. Tomorrow and yesterday sullen rain chills bones and floods unpaved streets. Fire and ice—the advantages of both may be obtained with ease in the black belt. Light, dark, white, black: a way of life blurs, and the focus shifts. Black, white, black: a rhythm ripples in the sun, pounds in steaming, stinking shacks, dances in the blood. Reality is kaleidoscopic in the black belt. Sometimes one's vision changes with it. A crooked man climbed a crooked tree on a crooked hill. Somewhere, in the midst of the past, a tenor sang of valleys lifted up and hills made low. Death at the heart of life, and life in the midst of death. The tree of life is indeed a Cross.

Darkly, incredibly, the interstate highway that had knifed through Virginia and the Carolinas narrowed and stopped. It was three o'clock in the morning and bitterly cold. We found it difficult to believe that we were actually back in the South. But in the twinkling of an eye our brave, clean highway became a backwoods Georgia road, deep in Cracker country, and we knew we were home. We were low on gas and miles from a point on the map, miles from sanctuary in Atlanta. We found a gas station and stopped. While one of us got the tank filled, the other went to the outdoor phone. Our Massachusetts plates seemed to glow in the night. As I shivered in the phone booth, I saw, through a window, white men turn and stare. Then my eye caught the sign over the door—WHITE ONLY. We had planned to get a Coke to keep us awake until Atlanta, but I guessed I no longer cared.

I heard the operator speak and then Father Scott in Atlanta. His voice was sleepy—and tired—and it took him a minute to recall our meeting at the airport a week or two before. Then he shifted into gear, and I received precise instructions. We would find a small street at the end of the night and a certain door. We would knock and say that Father Scott had said that we were to be admitted to the Canterbury House next door. There would be black faces and a warm floor, the Eucharist in the morning and coffee to send us on our way. What we found there we sometimes think we shall see again only in Heaven. The Love before Which we knelt in the morning would not again be visible at an altar, except to souls that had taken their first steps on the long trek out of the flesh. One cannot otherwise kneel in the real presence of a brother's hate, but that is to get ahead of our story. We drove on into the night. Incongruously, we came upon an all-night truckstop, midway to nowhere. There appeared to be no sign over the door, and I went in to get coffee-to-go. Too late, I discovered that hatred hadn't advertised—perhaps the sign had blown off in a storm. When I ordered the coffee, all other voices stopped. I turned from cold stares and fixed my gaze on a sign over the COUNTER: ALL CASH RECEIVED FROM SALES TO NIGGERS WILL BE SENT DIRECTLY TO THE UNITED KLANS OF AMERICA. I read it again and again, nausea rising swiftly and savagely, as the suspicious counterboy spilled coffee over the cups. It was lousy coffee. But worse than chicory was the taste of black men's blood. It was cheap: only twenty-five cents. At least Judas went for thirty.

It was high noon as we walked into the Selma Post Office to sign for a registered letter, and the lines at the windows were long. In the line next to me a redneck turned and stared: at my seminarian's collar, at my ESCRU button, at my face. He turned to a friend. "Know what he is?" The friend shouted "No." Resuming, the speaker whinnied, "Why, he's a white niggah." I was not happy thus to become the object of every gaze. And yet deep within me rose an affirmation and a tenderness and a joy that wanted to shout. Yes! If pride were appropriate in the ambiguities of my presence in Selma, I should be unspeakably proud of my title. For it is the highest honor, the most precious distinction

I have ever received. It is one that I do not deserve—and cannot ever earn. As I type now, my hands are hopelessly white. "But my *heart* is black. . . ." Oh, the drolleries one could spin! I *was* proud, for the redneck's contempt was the obverse of an identity and an acceptance that were very real, if still ambiguous, in another part of town. Hear, O Israel: given an irony or two in the holy mystery of His economy, I am indeed a "white nigger." I wouldn't swap the blessings He has given me. But *black* would be a very wonderful, a very beautiful color to be.

Bunnie sat astride my knee. She is four, the youngest of eleven (it would have been twelve, but there wasn't room for a premature black baby in the white hospital). She smiled, yet there was a hesitancy in her eyes. Her daddy smiled down at her and asked, "Do you love Jon?" Quietly but firmly, Bunnie said, "No." We had lived with Bunnie's family only a few days, and I was sure I knew what she meant. A part of me seemed to die inside, and I fought back tears. But there was nothing I could say, nothing I could do. Wisely, her daddy, who was already a very dear friend, did not pursue the matter. . . . When, a few days later, Bunnie pulled me down to her, cupped my face with her tiny hands and kissed me, I knew something very important (and incredibly beautiful) had happened. As Stringfellow says in *My People Is the Enemy*, "that is called a sacrament."

We had parked the car at the church. The rector had not been there, so we had strolled a block or two to the office of an attorney whom we had met at St. Paul's and encountered several times since. This time our visit was more cordial. We had given him and his wife a copy of *My People Is the Enemy* for Easter, and I think they were deeply touched. This time he was less suspicious, less defensive, less insistent that we "get the hell out of town." We had talked this time of the gospel, of what a white moderate could do when he discovered that the White Citizens' Council wasn't all-powerful, of certain changes in the school system that the grapevine said might be forthcoming. We left his office in a spirit of something very much like friendship. Something having to do with human hearts, something like the faith of the Church had been explored and shared with a white man in

the black belt. We gave thanks to the One Whom we had be-
sought as we stepped across the threshold of his office, and
quietly savored the glory of God as we strolled back to the car.
We stopped for a light, and a man got out of his car and approached us. He was dressed in a business suit and looked re-
spectable—this was not a redneck, so we could relax. He stopped
in front of us, inspecting us from head to toe. His eyes paused
for a moment at our ESCRU buttons and the collar. Then he
spoke, very quietly. "Are you the scum that's been going to the
Episcopal Church?" With a single voice we answered, "The scum,
sir?" "Scum," he returned, "S-C-U-M. That's what you are—you
and the nigger trash you bring with you." We replied as gently
as we could, "We can spell, sir. We're sorry you feel that way."
He turned contemptuously on his heel, and we crossed our street
sadly. Yet it was funny—riotously, hilariously, hideously funny!
We laughed all the way back home—at the man, at his cruelty, at
his stupidity, at our cleverness, at the success with which we had
suavely maintained "the Christian posture." And then, though we
have not talked about it, we both felt a little dirty. Maybe the
Incarnate God was truly present in that man's need and was asking us for something better than a smirk. (I started to say "more
truly *human* than a smirk." But I don't know about that. We are
beginning to believe deeply in original sin: theirs and ours.)

The judge, an Episcopalian and a racist, waited for us to
finish a nervous introduction. We had encountered him only too
often in his capacity as head usher, and we knew our man. Now
that we sat in his elegantly appointed office in the Dallas County
Courthouse, we were terrified. We knew what this man could do,
and what we had not seen ourselves, we had heard from our
friends among the high school kids. We concluded with something more-or-less coherent about the situation in St. Paul's. He
began: "You, Jonathan and Judy, will always be welcome in St.
Paul's." We smiled appreciatively. "But," he continued, "the
nigger trash you bring with you will *never* be accepted in St.
Paul's." We thought for an instant about the beautiful kids we
take with us every Sunday. Especially about Helen, the eldest
daughter in the first family who had opened their home and

hearts to us, a lovely, gentle, gracious girl who plans to enter nurse's training when she is graduated from high school this June. She must be one of the sweetest, prettiest girls in creation. Then anger rose in us—a feeling akin, I suppose, to the feeling of a white man for the sanctity of southern womanhood. Helen, trash? We should have left his office then, for we were no longer free men. Symbolically (a less symbolic phenomenon is real enough) he had raped our sister and friend. From that moment, we loathed the man—perhaps a bit more acutely than he loathed her. His sin—and ours. "The strategy of love" had already been lost. What, Lord Christ, does one do? Sometimes we do not know. Much later we told the judge that we thought the gospel, as it had been delivered to the Holy Catholic Church (of which we hoped the Episcopal Church was a part), rather specifically discouraged his notion that "our Episcopal Church is a white church." He answered that the gospel also forbade our living with Negroes, "since God made white men and black men separate and if He'd wanted them commingled He'd have made them all alike." We asked him to cite New Testament evidence. He replied that he wasn't talking about the gospel anyway, but about reality. He was quite clear that he knew God's thinking on this point, however. We then talked a bit about white supremacy and some of the means which had been used to achieve it. He denied that human slavery had had anything to do with it—and also that the beating of our kids on "Bloody Sunday" was any exception to his assertion that Negroes get more kindly treatment in the black belt than they do anywhere else in the country—and concluded that the real problem was federal intervention in the cotton industry, in voter registration, in the churches. Towards the end of the interview, the judge brought up the matter of the photographers who had accompanied the first group who had attempted to integrate the church. Though we had been energetically involved in the attempt, we, too, had not been entirely happy about the photographers. The judge insisted that we had brought them, which we denied. We made it clear that to an extent we sympathized with his objections. But he insisted on pursuing the point, claiming that since we were in the group we shared in the guilt of the group. Though we had not known that the photographers were with us until we got almost to the church, we agreed with the judge that we shared the "guilt" of the group. (It is not a guilt we lament particularly: the photographers made the moment an object of national concern, which was entirely appropriate.) Then we suggested that, by the same token, the judge himself was implicated in the injustice perpetrated against the Negro by the white men in Dallas County (actually, he is notorious on his own hook, even by the standards of white moderates in the county). With some belligerence, he replied that he was not, that he had spent all his life in Selma. We missed the point of the last and said: "Sir, you're a legal mind, trained to be consistent. Don't you see the inconsistency of what you've just said?" A crafty smile spread across the judge's face as he replied, "That's not inconsistent. That's the way we think here, those of us who have spent all our lives here and really know the situation." He had made the same point in several other contexts that only a southern white man who had never left the black belt could see things as they really are. His concluding remark was more concise than the home-style filibuster he had staged earlier (at a particularly crucial moment he had insisted on reading us page after page of a statistical school report): "I'm not guilty of anything. Only guilty men have trouble sleeping at night. I don't have any trouble sleeping." We could not suppress the retort that we thought maybe he should. In spite of ourselves, we went through the farce of shaking hands. As we had strolled to the courthouse, on our way to see the judge, we had recalled— only partly in jest—that "this kind does not come out, except by prayer and fasting."

When we got an Alabama plate for the car, we made the mistake of giving the Scotts' number in the federal project as our local address. In less than twenty-four hours, Mrs. Scott was notified by the project authorities that her house was being watched and would soon be inspected. If "those troublemakers at the Episcopal Church" or any of their luggage were found, the Scotts would be thrown out in the street. We moved out a little after midnight when the streets were dark and nearly deserted.

Fortunately, friends of the Scotts, who own their house in a Negro neighborhood on the edge of town, offered to take us in. Then we noticed that we were being followed uptown, especially when we drove away from the church. Mrs. Scott told us one evening that the police had been looking for "the people who've been going to the Episcopal Church." We discussed the situation with Bunnie's father, who felt that we were too remote in East Selma and insisted that we move in with his family. Now the telephone rings at six in the morning. When somebody finally stumbles out of bed to answer, there is only the sound of breathing at the other end.

When we moved in with our present family, we knew where Bunnie's mother stood. A few nights before, she had told us politely but emphatically that she didn't like white people—any white people. She knew from countless experiences that they couldn't be trusted. Until very recently, she would not have allowed white people to stay in her home. Though saddened, we were grateful for her honesty and told her so. We also told her that though we would understand if she didn't believe us, we had begun to love her and her family deeply. By the night we moved in, her reserve had almost disappeared. She was wonderfully hospitable to us, notwithstanding the suspicion she must still have felt. We spent an evening with Lonzie and Alice at the Elks' Club. Late in the evening a black nationalist approached her. "What are you doing here with them?" he asked. "They're white people." Much to our surprise and perhaps a little to her own, she answered: "Jon and Judy are my friends. They're staying in my home. I'll pick my own friends, and nobody'll tell me otherwise." The name for that, Brother Stringfellow, is *miracle*.

The girls looked particularly beautiful as we went into church on Palm Sunday. Their gloves and dresses were freshly cleaned and pretty. Their hairdos were lovely. There was a freshness, a quiet radiance about them which made us catch our breath. We were startled from our vision by a member of the congregation entering the church as we did. His greeting was unmistakable: "You god-damned scum. . . ."

The disappointments of Holy Week and the bitterness of

Easter Communion at St. Paul's—we assume you have seen a copy of our letter to Bishop Carpenter—forced our eyes back to the inscription over the altar: HE IS NOT HERE. FOR HE IS RISEN. In a dreadful parody of their meaning, the words seem to tell a grim truth that was not exhausted by their liturgical import.

This is the stuff of which our life is made. There are moments of great joy and moments of sorrow. Almost imperceptibly, some men grow in grace. Some men don't. Christian hope, grounded in the reality of Easter, must never degenerate into optimism. For that is the road to despair. Yet it ought never to conclude that because its proper end is Heaven, the Church may dally at its work until the End is in sight. The thought of the Church is fraught with tension because the life of the Church is *caught* in tension. For the individual Christian and the far-flung congregation alike, that is part of the reality of the Cross.

There are good men here, just as there are bad men. There are competent leaders and a bungler here and there. We have activists who risk their lives to confront a people with the challenge of freedom and a nation with its conscience. We have neutralists who cautiously seek to calm troubled waters. We have men about the work of reconciliation who are willing to reflect upon the cost and pay it. Perhaps at one time or another the two of us are all of these. Sometimes we take to the streets, sometimes we yawn through interminable meetings. Sometimes we talk with white men in their homes and offices, sometimes we sit out a murderous night with an alcoholic and his family because we love them and cannot stand apart. Sometimes we confront the posse, and sometimes we hold a child. Sometimes we stand with men who have learned to hate, and sometimes we must stand a little apart from them. Our life in Selma is filled with ambiguity, and in that we share with men everywhere. We are beginning to see as we never saw before that we are truly in the world and yet ultimately not of it. For through the bramble bush of doubt and fear and supposed success we are groping our way to the realization that above all else, we are called to be saints. That is the mission of the Church everywhere. And in this, Selma, Alabama, is like all the world: it needs the life and witness of militant *saints*.

Foreclosure of a Mortgage

Reflections from a Point
on the
Way of the Cross
A Meditation in Theological Ethics

It is unnecessary to say that the question of violence is fraught with ambiguity for the Church. This is so, partly because the question of violence is a representative question: in a very basic way it involves the Church's understanding of the gospel She proclaims, and it involves the lives and the welfare of all of us, whether we stand within or without the Church. For many reasons, some pastoral, some historical, the Church knows that Her response to the question affects not only Her own life, but that of far distant ramparts of Western civilization. As if this were not cause enough for ambiguity, the question of violence is related to many other issues which themselves are far from settled in the mind of the Church. Scripture, theology, politics, economics—all raise questions that often seem to justify ethical ambivalence.

The position developed in this paper rests upon a number of presuppositions which ought to be acknowledged at the outset. Perhaps the first is that the presuppositions are vastly more significant than any conceivable consequence that might follow from them. The outermost branches of the argument, however interesting to the eye—and ultimately important for decision and action—are nevertheless incidental to the roots. Too often the roots remain hidden until the discussion is far-spent. At some point, past yawning, the combatants in debate generously agree that their difficulties hinge perhaps on divergent premises and jovially retire into amiable somnolence. Premises usually make a difference.

In deference to convention, the writer will avoid the personal pronoun like the plague. But he hopes, for the sake of fairness, that when he says "the Christian," "the disciple," or "the Church" it is understood that he does not presume to confuse his own commitment with the acknowledged mind of the

Church. Yet, it goes perhaps without saying, if he did not conceive his task ultimately to be the proclamation of the gospel, he might possibly prefer silence to the sound of his own voice.

As the Church faces the question of violence, it is important that She begin with Her baptism. The Church Militant is not thereby automatically an association of militarists; nor is She primarily and essentially a pacifist society. She is the Church, the holy Body of those who have been baptized into the Lord's death and resurrection, who in Him and with Him have been crucified and raised from death and lifted up in unspeakable glory to the right hand of the Father. If She is to be faithful to Her own nature as the continuing physical manifestation of the Incarnation, this supposition must be fundamental to all that She thinks or does. It would be difficult to overemphasize this. If the Church allows any other presupposition to usurp its place in Her self-consciousness, She is doomed to a position (whatever it may be) that is anomalous at best. Though the reverse has probably been more frequently the case in history, it is possible for the Church to be "right" for the wrong reasons. The Church is not only metaphorically, but actually and existentially the Body of Christ: She is not "a religion," partaking in the defining characteristics of a class, but specifically, uniquely the organic union of men and women who have been made members of the Incarnate Lord. And He is the One Who was crucified, Who has been raised from the dead, and Who now reigns in glory. That defines for us, as Churchmen, our manhood and our Godhead.

Men who have been baptized into the death and resurrection of Jesus Christ know one allegiance to One Sovereignty that precedes all others. With all regard for HUAC and the D.A.R., the Christian is first a servant of the Kingdom and only then a nationalist. The ambiguities of biblical revelation notwithstanding, he is committed to the Life and teaching of Jesus Christ: indeed, he can no longer claim any existence independent of That Life and teaching. In any given situation, whether problematic or relatively uncomplicated, the disciple seeking to be faithful in all things will feel a responsibility to assess alternative goals, motives, and actions in terms of the highest obedience he can conceive. This tautology is not trivial if one supposes that though there may be quantitative proximity if not equivalence between "the highest good" and "the lesser evil," the subjective experience of the moral agent will be qualitatively very different under the two categories. Both mood and motivation will vary, depending upon whether one is attempting to avoid the greatest evil or attain the highest good.

In the light of his response to the outreaching Love of God, the Christian will know only one motivation in his thinking and dreaming and acting that is ultimately legitimate and unambiguously authentic. That is *agapé*. When the Christian first begins to answer with his own feeble love the overwhelming Love of God, he finds himself animated by an attitude that is equally "holy obedience" and "perfect freedom." In that freedom which is holy obedience, the Christian has only one principle, only one agenda. And that is the dynamic of life-in-response to the loving, judging, healing, merciful revelation by God Himself of His holy will.

It is pertinent—and salutary—to ask how the Christian *knows* the revelation of God's gracious purpose. Christian writers too often ground arguments allusively in "revelation" without the illumination of concrete epistemology. The Christian sustained within the broadstream of the traditional teaching of the Church finds in Scripture an authentic medium of God's Self-disclosure. God reveals Himself to us ultimately in the complex, integrated, organic, Personal "event" of Jesus Christ. That Event is narrated for us first in the New Testament—though the narration continues, with painful ambiguity, in the life of the Church. At any rate, the orthodox Christian looks with confidence to the Bible, and especially to the New Testament, for concrete documentation of the Life in Which he is grounded. In the recorded witness of the primitive Church to the life and teaching and total ministry of Her Lord, Churchmen of all ages find the authoritative model for an integrated life which for convenience we divide into "doctrine" and "ethics" and "worship." The continuing search for and appropriation of the Divine model by the individual Christian is conducted within the Church, under the guidance and illumination of the Holy Spirit. The operations of the Holy Spirit are no less significant for the Christian than the biblical records, though in practice we sometimes tend to minimize this in the more structured outposts of Christendom. There is an authentically Pentecostal note in the chant of civil rights workers in the black belt, "I'm gonna *do* what the Spirit says 'Do,' " which the Church, in Her regard for order and authority, cannot afford to neglect. This is not to overlook the ambiguities of the workings of the Holy Spirit. It is simply to recall that Scripture itself guarantees to Christians the eschatological significance of the decisive, existential, Spirit-filled "moment." In the history of the Church there is a fine balance between the constitutive and the charismatic. The evidence of Holy Scripture and the inner prompting and testimony of the Holy Spirit always operate in a dialectical relationship, and the consequent tension is intrinsic to the life of the Church.

It remains to say only that the Christian is obligated-in-freedom to submit every historical issue, every historical decision to the eschatological dialectic cited above. He is thus liberated, to one degree or another, from the "given" in the world-view of his culture. It goes without saying that just as it is possible (alas) for the "religionist" to be blind to empirical reality, it is equally possible for him to be the slave of historical conditions. The Christian is delivered from both afflictions. Life in the world as it is—and Life in the Spirit. Christians are truly in the world and yet ultimately not of it. That is one of the paradoxes—and incomparable blessings—of the Incarnation. The Christian stands with a foot planted *firmly* in two worlds. Yet I think he must hope that one leg will grow a little disproportionately in strength and so come to bear more of his weight. The Resurrection and Ascension are paradigmatic, too.

It is generally agreed among Christian writers that "war" is contrary to the recorded teachings of Jesus. It is agreed that, at least on an absolute and perhaps abstract plane, physical violence is incompatible with the Sermon on the Mount. Beyond this, there is little agreement. Among the various types of pacifists and between pacifists and nonpacifists there are enormous differences with regard to interpretation of Jesus' teaching, with regard to the applicability of Jesus' teaching to the exigencies of historical situations, and with regard to kinds and degrees of violence.

Writers defending radically different positions vis-à-vis the use of force will nevertheless profess common sympathy with presuppositions summarized in the prolegomena above. There are significant differences in motivation and methodology; what one man espouses on principle, another chooses merely as strategy. It may well seem, therefore, that it is scarcely possible to obtain an objective grasp on the problem. The ensuing discussion, very much a "private affair" in a sense, is not intended to be either broadly relevant or widely appealing. It is offered with the hope, however, that it will come to terms with some of the issues that divide men who work from *agapé* as the lowest *acceptable* common denominator. The writer joins in the virtually universal assumption, perhaps itself an illusion, that they are not insoluble.

There are many kinds of violence. There is the contemporary phenomenon of "total war," in which both "aggressor" and "defender" resort to massive and undifferentiated destruction. There is "limited war," in which the parties in conflict either do not have the capacity for total war or lack the inclination for it. Within a reasonably sophisticated war machinery there are rather sharply delineated procedures—to oversimplify a bit—for "strategic," "tactical," and "guerrilla" warfare. There is the refinement, frequently endorsed by pacifists, which we call "international police action." There are wars of aggression and wars-to-end-war, revolutions and counterrevolutions, wars of acquisition and "peace-keeping" procedures. There were the Crusades.

The several kinds of war do not exhaust the forms of violence sanctioned in society. There is local police action. There are capital punishment for criminals and corporal punishment for children. There are various forms of psychological coercion, which, though they do not directly involve physical violence, nevertheless require methods which trouble the Christian's conscience and can be justified only as "violating a person for his own good."

The man committed, in Christ, to *agapé* as an irreducible minimum (both as a principle and as a method for "realizing" the Kingdom) is anguished at the moral dilemma occasioned by all the forms of violence perpetrated in society. He may be less disturbed by the sanctioned forms than by crimes of violence—which are, of course, not under discussion here—but he is inescapably concerned by any violation of persons. His suffering is inevitable, whether he reluctantly endorses some or all of the sanctioned forms of violence as the only available means in a given situation of implementing *agapé* or eschews them all as hopelessly tainted. Gandhi and Forsyth would find, I suspect, little on which to disagree at *this* point. The Christian pacifist and the Christian nonpacifist would both (at their best) ascribe their decisions and policies to the motivation of redemptive love. It is the assumption of this discussion, then, that it is here that one must locate the fundamental issue for Christian theological-ethics. The present writer is unwilling, at any rate, to consider the question from any other perspective: to do so would contradict the presuppositions established in the prolegomena. The Christian is not bidden to love when he can or when it is convenient and expedient for him to do so, but to love as the Father has first loved him. The question may be stated simply thus: What methods are open to redemptive love as means of adjudicating and resolving social conflict? Or, more narrowly, what alternatives are closed to the Christian by his profession of obedience? The two questions are linked, of course, with a third: Are there situations in which Christian obedience-in-freedom entails either civil disobedience or "conscientious objection" to the policies and methods of the state?

Christian pacifists and nonpacifists alike, as well as humanists and writers of other essentially secular orientations, are saying with increasing urgency that *total* war in the "thermo-nuclear age" is no longer a rational possibility for resolving international conflicts. There are indications even within the Communist bloc of reluctance to engage in the total warfare for which many nations now have the capacity. Though it remains a real enough possibility, the issues it raises are so unsubtle that discussion seems unnecessary. Indeed, the issues are less moral than practical. The fundamental question is not of altruism, but of human survival. Despite the portion of American defense spending allocated to massive retaliation, there are an increasing number of advocates of renewed concentration on our capacity for limited warfare. The debatable issues raised for the Christian by the possibility of total war may, at any rate, be more fruitfully discussed under categories that involve greater ethical ambiguity. Whatever the moral intricacies of more limited forms of warfare, the Church can scarcely advocate wholesale obliteration of masses of nationals whose culpability cannot be assessed. Whether the Christian can in any way be avoidably involved in such obliteration is a question that he might well prefer to contemplate in a prison rather than in a cockpit or behind a control panel.

Though to do so is perhaps arbitrary, I shall dismiss the question of acquisitive wars of aggression with a reference to the Trapp family, who left Nazi Germany for the mountains of Vermont. For the Baron, as well as for many others, there could be no hesitation; it was painfully clear to him that as a Catholic he could under no circumstances accept the offered command of one of Hitler's U-boats. If Bonhoeffer's attitude toward flight seems ethically superior, Baron Trapp's decision against participation in aggression has not found opposition among American nonpacifist moral theologians. One must add parenthetically that should the Nazi German and the American positions ever be reversed, it would be interesting to note whether any Baron Trapps could be found among us. Unfortunately, space does not permit discussion of the numerous ambiguities which surround this question. The Allied attitude toward "war guilt" is awesomely illogical. Suffice it to say that with regard to the instance at hand, it is reasonably clear from the study of historians of the period that, more than any other single factor, Allied behavior at Versailles can account for Hitler's initial rise to power. Yet across the land, pulpits confidently expressed nausea at the Nazi affront to acutely sensitive consciences. If one is at all inclined to cynicism, it is perhaps amusing to recall the history of American response to Nazi aggression. But that is another story.

It is perhaps on the question of defensive or retaliatory war that the Christian is most painfully confronted. Even with the motive of revenge theoretically removed, it is difficult to see how he can justify the return of violence for violence. It is assumed, of course, that the Christian does not engage in aggression. But it is often forgotten that, again by definition as it were, he has taken upon himself-in-Christ the aggressor's burden of need, hatred, fear, hostility, cruelty. The Church too often preaches the Sermon on the Mount as a virtually *irrelevant* "eschatological impossibility"—if not with tongue in cheek, which of course is far worse. When one gets through saying that Jesus consistently talks about the Kingdom proleptically, it is all too easy to conclude that He is impractical as well. In the final analysis, "radical eschatology" is for the End—*not for now*. And thus we forget in the Church that under the conditions of historical existence, in the space-and-time of a fallen world, *we have been baptized into the Lord's death and resurrection*. Nothing could be more radical or impossible or impractical or unrealistic. But that is precisely what has already happened. There are saintly men and women within the Church who have not allowed the preaching from Her pulpits to discourage them. Though they have been taught with the rest of us that the eschatological perfection of the Sermon on the Mount is so far above and beyond them that they can scarcely hope to approximate it, they nevertheless continue to pray for Grace. Sometimes the approximation is closer than it is supposed to be, and we call them "saints." And sometimes when we call them "saints" we sound as if we rejoice in our "ordinariness"—by which we imply, perhaps, that some of us are called to be saints and some, sinners. It is instructive to reread from time to time the "Promises" from the Ministration of Holy Baptism. To accept the calling of a Christian is to accept the vocation of sanctity.

The "local color" of the Sermon on the Mount is, as a matter of fact, less eschatological than embarrassingly mundane. Altars, prisons, a man's lust for a woman, divorces, cloaks, and beggars: these are all familiar phenomena in a world we know. It is unlikely, from the events of Holy Week, that the world of Palestine in our Lord's lifetime found the "ethics of the Kingdom" any less radical—or offensive—than contemporary society evidently does. Certainly it can come to the Church as no surprise that some of Her ways are objectionable to the society in which She tries to minister. The early Church, at any rate, was often made to absorb the "surprise" in Her very flesh. This She did, in obedience to Her Lord, without either individual or collective retaliation.

The Sermon on the Mount, the Cross, and the cruciform experience of the early Church are paradigmatic of active (rather than "passive") *nonresistance* to evil. This, as we shall see below in discussion of nonviolent social revolution, raises a significant question for the Christian activist. With respect to the issue at hand, the thrust of the Sermon, the Cross, and the witness of the martyrs denies violent retaliation to the Christian as a legitimate mode of loving redemptively.

The question here is not one of effectiveness, nor of immediate practicability, but of obedience to the claims of the gospel. The Christian's profession of faith thus puts him in an insoluble bind. We do not live in a theocracy, but in a "mixed" culture, in which Christians, religionists of other professions, and pagans are all bound together in mutual interdependence under a "system" which reflects the interests and convictions of them all. Saint and sinner lean upon each other for survival—and not infrequently for support in the implementation of their several convictions. In a "post-Christian" civilization, with the heritage that appellation implies, the Church and the world are subtly as well as superficially commingled. Within that civilization, all have complicated loyalties and mutual obligations (whether acknowledged or not). In a crisis situation, such as a national or regional depression or natural disaster, the organicity of society is starkly revealed.

The Church, dimly conscious at least, of the ambiguities in Her history, is becoming increasingly if belatedly aware of Her apostolic commitment to the constant renewal of Her evangelical dialogue *with* and participation *in* the world which engulfs Her. Though Her influence (for better or worse) is enormous in some quarters, it has been virtually exhausted in others. The missionary enterprise demands continual reappraisal at all levels of the theological complex by which it is sustained. In these fascinating days of our history, the repercussions of reappraisal are indeed shaking the framework to its foundations.

The intolerable tensions which threaten to disintegrate the sensitive Christian emerge in agonizing questions. What does missionary involvement mean in this, now that, situation? How, on the one hand, does the Christian manifest his relevance and his concern for the world about him and yet bear faithful witness, on the other hand, to the gospel which constitutes his relevance? How does he honestly and realistically fill out the sufferings of the Incarnate Lord under the ambiguous conditions of historical existence, without overzealously compromising His holiness? How, when his conscience and his loyalties are divided by the breadth of his compassion, does he correlate the scriptural witness to the Holy One's Self-disclosure in history with the coursing stream of history in which he presently seeks by faith to discern the continuing activity of the same loving, redemptive, judging, saving Sovereign Will?

With regard to the discussion at hand, the Christian will apprehend his vocation in part as a corollary of where he locates the stress in the reversible equation of Divine transcendence and immanence. If he leans to the latter, he will plunge into the rapids of immediate history, trusting that the Holy Spirit will guide him through its perplexities. He will stress the prophetic imperative for active involvement and place a high value on effectiveness and proximate success. If, with the writer, he leans to the former, he will tend to discern the redemptive activity of God in history as it tallies with the tradition(s) of His Self-disclosure in the corporate experience of those who know themselves as His people. Though he anticipates (and awaits) a Consummation of history—not a denial, but an ultimate affirmation and redemption of history—he will be acutely conscious of the ambiguities in the structure of things, of the fact that though Creation is the glorious gift of loving and holy Hands, history is truly fallen and tainted with a disease which finally only those Hands can cure. In, toward, and *for* that history, he will see his vocation, always with humility and repentance, as being the Presence of the Living Christ. Not the Wrath of God (which will always be only too real for him), but the active, critical, redeeming compassion of the Lord Jesus will be his model and the ground of his witness. As he finds in the world the way of the Cross, he will bear forever in his heart the lovely hymn of the God-bearer. For the prophetic reality of that song of songs, and for the gracious possibility of his own unworthy participation in it, he will give unending thanks. And he will learn at last that it is not his own contribution to the enterprise which is important (though it *is* important), but that of the One Whose Name is Holy. And perhaps his prophetic speech and prophetic motions, learned at the Virgin's knee, will sometimes reflect obversely the temptations he has encountered in the Way.

"He hath put down the mighty from their seat, and hath exalted the humble and meek. He hath filled the hungry with good things; and the rich he hath sent empty away." So the lyric of radical upheaval, of social and political and economic revolution, the world-breaking, world-shaping utterance of Amos and his heirs echoes in Mary's glad song. Her Son was a son of the poor. He got the treatment the poor have often gotten.

One is inclined to make a connection between Jesus' second reply to Pilate in the Fourth Gospel ("My kingship is not of this world; if my kingship were of this world, my servants would fight, that I might not be handed over to the Jews; but my kingship is not from the world.") and certain of His remarks in the Synoptics. The first of the "Beatitudes" and the *mashal* about the camel's prospect of getting through the eye of a needle will do. The connection here is not primarily related to the *inability* of the poor to take effective action in their own behalf, though realism is by no means irrelevant. The point is rather that the poor are strategically situated, as it were, to stumble into the way of the Cross. Witness the workers in Birmingham a century ago (Dickens was not a fool, for all his sentimentality) and the Negroes of the black belt.

With the advent of labor unionism and the movement for racial justice (to stick with the illustration above), some of the poor have begun to find the Way obscure. That is neither surprising nor, from another perspective, entirely lamentable. As Bishop Newbigin says somewhere in a missions journal, many of the directions in which contemporary Western (secular) culture is moving are refractions of the eschatology of the Church. Refraction seems always to involve corruption, and many of the methods and means (and perhaps the motives) of organized attempts at securing social justice appear in a dubious light to the Christian. Yet "all things work together for good for those who love God," and the Christian discerns in all the ambiguities of social ferment the operations of a familiar Hand. For this, too, he is thankful—and chastened. If he is reminded of Cyrus, he can only repent for the failure of the Church to be Herself. Yet he cannot precisely *be* Cyrus; his name is Israel. The Lord Jesus did not say "stab the oppressor" (or even "lie down in the street"), but "go a second mile" and "give your cloak also." How, then, does the Christian respond? How—a not so subtly different question—does the Christian whose cultural experience lies with the middle class, who is impelled by the prophetic vision of the Virgin's song to identify with the life and cause of the poor, make his stand in faithful obedience to the Life of the Cross?

"When the days drew near for him to be received up, he set his face to go to Jerusalem." The entire pericope of the Samaritan Villagers, from the Lucan "special section," is evocative. Perhaps it provides a clue for the troubled Christian whose sympathies lie with the social revolution(s) of our times, but who finds each of the several strands (and himself!) short-circuited in Jesus' gloriously paradoxical combination of prophet, messianic king, and suffering servant.

It is not precisely true to say that Jesus died for the poor, any more than that he fought for social justice or, for that matter, relied upon coercion to change the hearts of men. Yet (fortunately) the "interim" has been longer—and will probably be vastly longer still—than (equally fortunately) He had thought. We have had time to perceive the integrity of the Beatitudes and the Cross and the Ascension, of Prophet, Priest, and King. And so we, too, may set our faces to go to Jerusalem, as He has gone before us: ". . . to preach good news to the poor . . . to proclaim release to the captives and recovering of sight to the blind, to set at liberty those who are oppressed, to proclaim the acceptable year of the Lord." Like Him, we seek Jerusalem "not to destroy men's lives but to save them." We go to make our witness to the truth that has set us free. We go to stand with the captives and the blind and the oppressed. We go in "active nonresistance," not to "confront," but to love and to heal and to free. Our motives must be loving and our methods, chaste. Otherwise, the means of "proclaiming" open to us know no bounds but those of our own imagination and initiative.

Whether the Christian "demonstrates" in a picket line or "boycotts" an oppressor must depend upon whether the action is undertaken vindictively and coercively. If his protest is an act of contrition, he may act with confidence.

"He set his face to go to Jerusalem." One cannot go to Jerusalem with the song of Mary on one's lips and in one's heart without finding enemies. Between deliberate provocation and passivity there is a middle course for compassion and truth. To find it, of course, one must *be* in Jerusalem. And one must pray for strength to carry a cross. That done, lo the Presence, and a living sacrifice of praise and thanksgiving.

June 22, 1965

Many times since my reconversion three years ago I have been asked (with varying degrees of outrage and pain), "Why?" I have found that the best way to answer has been to tell a story, to sing a "song of myself," which, like that of the singer, finally modulated to the Song of Songs: the Eternal Word of God. Intellectual history had to wait for flesh to tell its tale. That in itself was a great lesson for me.

Before I left for Selma the second time, a kind friend asked me some day to "theologize my experience in Selma." At the time the phrase meant something to me: "self-righteousness," though I had yet to learn that. I was, of course, delighted. Since then a kind of song has sung itself in Selma (and in Cambridge), as a consequence of which the phrase now seems unmanageably abstract. I shall therefore sing the song instead, a few bars of it —and hope the Truth will out.

At two o'clock in the afternoon of March eighth, I dashed into the TV room of the Episcopal Theological School for an Executive Committee meeting. As I grabbed a cup of coffee and found a seat, I had just time to overhear one of the brethren say that his wife planned to fly down, before the chairman called the meeting to order. At some point on the agenda past yawning, the brother whose wife was flying was encouraged to make his pitch. There was trouble in Selma, as we all knew from

Huntley-Brinkley, and Dr. King had asked for northern volunteers. *That* was where his wife was flying, and he was trying to raise money for her travel expenses. A strategy was speedily devised for that purpose, and as we went our several ways there was excited talk about the possibility of sending other members of the community.

I raced back to Lawrence Hall, flew up the three flights, and hurled myself into the room of a friend. The friend had been asleep, but graciously composed himself for what was visibly my latest insanity. I delicately reminded him that he had invited me to go south with him over the spring holidays (to talk with Bishop Allin of Mississippi and others) and suggested that we go *now*. My friend was not free to go, and I went off to study, a little disconsolate. From time to time I mused: could I spare the time? Did I want to spare the time? Did He want . . . ? Reluctantly I admitted to myself that the idea was impractical, and, with a faintly tarnished feeling, I tucked in an envelope my contribution to the proposed "Selma fund."

"My soul doth magnify the Lord, and my spirit hath rejoiced in God my Saviour." I had come to Evening Prayer as usual that evening, and as usual I was singing the Magnificat with the special love and reverence I have always felt for Mary's glad song. "He hath showed strength with his arm." As the lovely hymn of the God-bearer continued, I found myself peculiarly alert, suddenly straining toward the decisive, luminous, Spirit-filled "moment" that would, in retrospect, remind me of others—particularly of one at Easter three years ago. Then it came. "He hath put down the mighty from their seat, and hath exalted the humble and meek. He hath filled the hungry with good things." I knew then that I must go to Selma. The Virgin's song was to grow more and more dear in the weeks ahead.

After a week-long, rain-soaked vigil at the "Berlin Wall," we still stood face to face with the Selma police, who were flanked by the sheriff's posse and backed by five or six ranks of state police. The President had not yet addressed the nation, and we were not a foot nearer the Dallas County Courthouse. I stood, for a change, in the front rank, ankle-deep in an enormous puddle flooding one side of the street. To my immediate right were high school students, for the most part, and further to the right were a swarm of clergymen. My end of the line surged forward at one point, led by a militant Episcopal priest whose temper (as usual) was at combustion-point. Thus I found myself only inches from a young policeman. The air crackled with tension and frustration and open hostility. Emma Jean, a sophomore in the Negro high school, who had been standing next to me before the line moved forward, called my name from behind. I reached back for her hand to bring her up to the front rank, but she did not see. Again she called, a note of growing concern in her voice, and asked me to come back before I got hurt. My determination had become infectiously savage, and I insisted that she come forward—I would not retreat! Again I reached for her hand, this time successfully, and pulled her forward. The young policeman spoke: "You're dragging her through the puddle. You ought to be ashamed for treating a girl like that." Flushing—I had forgotten the puddle—I snarled something at him about whose-fault-it-really-was, that managed to be both defensive and self-righteous. We matched baleful glances and then both looked away. And then came a moment of shattering internal quiet, in which I felt shame, indeed, and a kind of reluctant love for the young policeman. I apologized to Emma Jean. And then it occurred to me to apologize to *him* and to thank him. Though he looked away in contempt—I was not altogether sure I blamed him—I had received a blessing I would not forget. Before long the kids were singing "I love ———," filling in with the badge numbers of the policemen standing in front of us. The young policeman had apparently forgotten his badge, so one of my friends asked another for his name. His name was Charlie, which for some reason (Steinbeck, perhaps!) endeared him to me all the more. When we sang for him, he blushed and then smiled in a truly sacramental mixture of embarrassment and pleasure and shyness. Soon the young policeman looked relaxed, we all lit cigarettes (in a couple of instances, from a common match), and small groups of kids and policemen clustered to joke or talk cautiously about the situation. It was thus a shock later to look across the rank at the clergymen and their opposites, who glared across a still unbroken "Wall" in what appeared to be silent hatred. Had I been freely arranging the order for Evening Prayer that night, I think I might have followed the General Confession directly with the General Thanksgiving—or perhaps the Te Deum.

I was prepared for a tiresome crop of sermons as I entered St. Paul's Episcopal Church in Selma on Good Friday for the interdenominational "Seven Last Words." Most were as bad, in fact, as I had expected. One, on the other hand, was unforgettable. Dr. Newton, the pastor of the largest Presbyterian Church in Selma, himself an integrationist, preached about the word, "I thirst." The point of his meditation was that Jesus had had the humility and the freedom to ask for water *from His enemies.*

We were made to sit in our pew at the rear of St. Paul's Episcopal Church in Selma on Easter Sunday (yards from the nearest communicants) until everybody else had communicated and returned to their seats. When finally we were allowed to approach the altar, the looks and gestures of hostility we encountered on the way were palpable. Though I had tried to make careful and foresighted preparation, I found myself falling prey to the reigning dynamics. Then it occurred to me that if I could not go to the altar in genuine charity, in chaste compassion, then I would go only to my peril. For by my very presence I had assumed responsibility for "the weaker brethren." I had heard— and probably made—scornful remarks about the "validity" of *any* celebration at St. Paul's. Now "validity" was an existential and decisive question: but the validity in question was entirely my own. I could not make my Communion without sorrow under the circumstances. But I had begun to taste joy and perhaps the triumph of the Cross.

The night before Judy Upham, my fellow student from the Episcopal Theological School, and I left for the North we were the dinner guests of the priests and brothers at the Edmundite (Negro) mission. After dinner we withdrew with Father Ouellet, the pastor, to his living room. Our friend began to talk deeply and openly of his experience and of his life in Selma in particular. We were stunned at the honesty, the integrity, and the beauty of this saintly man. Though he graciously provided opportunities for us to talk, to share with him our concerns and beliefs and observations, it became increasingly clear to us that we could have little to say to the pain and the quiet glory of that life except that we revered and loved him. He said that after twelve years in Selma, he had finally stopped hating. Perhaps it was merely because he was nearing forty, but his bitterness had gone. Though (as a "white nigger") he had been repeatedly rebuffed by the white Protestant clergymen in town (and, presumably, by the pastor of the white Catholic Church, as well, though Father Ouellet himself is white), he thought it was time to try again to establish some sort of relationship with them all.

Father Ouellet said at some point early in the evening that he had discovered what the ecumenical movement was all about when he began to notice our faces in the congregation at Mass each Sunday (we had gotten into the habit of picking up the kids in the Negro family with whom we stayed after early Communion at St. Paul's Episcopal Church and taking them out to St. Elizabeth's Roman Catholic Church). As we knelt for his blessing before we left and he placed his hands on our heads, we knew that, from almost any perspective, a miracle had occurred.

As we packed the car our last day in Selma to return to seminary, my eye caught a number of times on the Alabama license tag. Each time, it occurred to me that—at some point on our route—it might be expedient to dig out Judy's Massachusetts plates. Yet I could not bring myself to remove the blue-and-orange tag which, in an ambivalent fashion, I had come to love. It may have been only that my first memories are of the towns in Kentucky and Arkansas where my family lived during World War II, and the fact that I had been graduated from a college in Virginia. At any rate, I could not remove the tag.

When we left Washington on the Baltimore Belt, an attractive Negro couple in a glistening new black Chevy pulled out behind us and shot by. As they passed, they both turned and stared. I nodded to them and tried to return their gaze. But instead I found myself flushing under their cool stare, and I quickly looked away. In their eyes, my identity was painfully clear. I wanted to shout to them, "No, no! I'm *not* an Alabama white. I'm on *your* side." We rode for a few miles in deeply troubled silence. There were no words that could dispel the pain and the shame and the vicarious guilt we both felt. Then, gently, illumination came. Of course, I could not shout, "No, no!" That would be cheap, cutting a knot that, in the ambiguous conditions of fallen creation, is far too sacred for minor surgery. To be a Christian, to be baptized into the Death-and-Life of the Cross, is not that simple. Whether we had known it or not, whether we liked it or not, whether it made any difference or not, we were in *His Name* and for *His sake* on the Baltimore Beltway, in Cambridge, Massachusetts, in Keene, New Hampshire, with "the Heart of Dixie" branded on our flesh and buried in our hearts. We were "standing in" for the rector at Selma and for the whole parish family at St. Paul's, for the white men of the black belt. Their guilt was ours, and ours, theirs. That was part of the covenant we had silently made with them when we had discovered that our "presence" in Selma meant listening and absorbing before it meant talking. We now knew that "chaste compassion" meant more than absorbing the suspicion and the fear and the hostility of our white brethren in Selma, though all that was part of the covenant, part of the price a Yankee Christian had better be prepared to pay if he goes to the black belt. It meant absorbing their guilt as well and suffering the cost which they might not yet even know was there to be paid. If, in Selma, our baptism made us "white niggers," we now knew that it also made us "Alabama whites." I suspect that knowledge lies very close to the heart of the harsh tenderness of the Cross, the costly, puzzling, eucharistic glory of the Tree of Life. It is certainly part of what Christians mean by "Atonement."

The discovery of all this has led to some unexpectedly beautiful moments. At the conclusion of my talk to the churchwomen of my home parish in New Hampshire some weeks ago, a militant liberal expressed the wish that I would stop calling the parishioners of St. Paul's, Selma, "Christians"—"churchmen" would make her happier. Instinctively, I felt defensive for the people of my adopted "parish family," recalling the painful ambivalence and anguished perplexity I knew some of them were beginning (belatedly, it is true—for all of us) to feel. Then I recalled some of the self-righteous insanities I permitted myself to indulge in, early in my life in Selma. Before I delivered a gentle blast I could not help thanking Him for the gift of delicious irony. "He chasteneth whom He loveth."

It was my great privilege during graduation this spring to help host the family of a very dear friend from the Deep South. For some reason, whether blessed or demonic I am still not entirely sure, they were bombarded by the language of civil rights, which seemed to be a theme in the week's festivities. During the sermon the afternoon before graduation—a particularly massive assault, it seemed—I became so uncomfortable for them that I stole to their pew to sit with them. I shall never forget the community which existed between us in that moment. The unspoken "wall" which had subtly divided us until then suddenly afforded a narrow path, and a thread of genuine affection ran through the fabric of our mutual disagreement and suspicion. Atonement is objective, indeed.

All of this is the raw material for living theology. And yet in as deep a sense, from my point of view, it is the *product* of living theology. The doctrines of the creeds, the enacted faith of the sacraments, were the essential precondition of the experience itself. The faith with which I went to Selma has not *changed*: it has grown. Darkening coals have kindled. Faith has taken wing and flown with a song in its wings. "My soul doth magnify the Lord, and my spirit hath rejoiced in God my Saviour."

I lost fear in the black belt when I began to know in my bones and sinews that I had truly been baptized into the Lord's death and Resurrection, that in the only sense that really matters I am already dead, and my life is hid with Christ in God. I began to lose self-righteousness when I discovered the extent to which my behavior was motivated by worldly desires and by the self-seeking messianism of Yankee deliverance! The point is simply, of course, that one's motives are usually mixed—and one had better know it. It occurred to me that though I was reasonably certain that I was in Selma because the Holy Spirit had sent me there, there nevertheless remained a fundamental distinction between my will and His. "And *Holy* is His Name." I was reminded by the Eucharist, by the daily offices, by the words of confession, by the healing judgment of the Spirit, that I am called *first* to holiness. Every impulse, every motive, every will under heaven must attend first to that if it is to be healthy and free within the ambiguities and tilted structures of a truly fallen Creation. "W*orldly* holiness," a dear friend of mine would rightly insist: but the *holiness*, the "chaste compassion" of the One in Whom all life, all love, all truth are grounded. Of the ubiquitous Kingship of the eternal Word, through Whom all things were made, I found very real if ambiguous confirmation in that beloved community who ate and slept and cursed and prayed in the rain-soaked streets of the Negro "compound" that first week in Selma.

Another kind of organicity has dawned upon me more gradually. As Judy and I said the daily offices day by day, we became more and more aware of the living reality of the invisible "communion of saints"—of the beloved community in Cambridge who were saying the offices, too, and sending us carbon copies of their notes (and a thousand other things as well!), of the ones gathered around a near-distant throne in Heaven—who blend with theirs our faltering songs of prayer and praise. With them, with black men and white men, with all of life, in Him Whose Name is above all the names that the races and nations shout, whose Name is Itself the Song Which fulfills and "ends" all songs, we are indelibly, unspeakably *one*.